The
Positive Attitude Development Workbook

Assimilating, Accommodating, Acclimating to Change

DEVELOPED BY **Lyle Wildes**

WITH **Joe Kelly**

WHOLE PERSON ASSOCIATES
DULUTH, MINNESOTA

Whole Person Associates, Inc.
210 West Michigan
Duluth, MN 55802-1908   218-727-0500
E-mail: books@wholeperson.com
Web site: http://www.wholeperson.com

The Positive Attitude Development Workbook
Assimilating, Accommodating, Acclimating to Change

Printed in the United States of America

10 9 8 7 6 5 4 3 2 1

Editor: Peg Johnson
Art Director: Joy Dey

Library of Congress Control Number: 2008911094
ISBN-13 978-1-57025-228-0
ISBN   1-57025-228-0

 **WHOLE PERSON ASSOCIATES**
210 West Michigan
Duluth, MN 55802-1908

Contents

Introduction

Dedicated to John and Lyn Clark Pegg

How to use this workbook

This workbook helps you learn the basics of *Positive Attitude Development (PAD)*. You can use it on your own or use it as a tool in a *PAD* group.

The introduction gives you an overall sense of our perspective on *Positive Attitude Development*. The chapters are designed to be read and used in order, since each chapter builds on concepts in the previous chapter(s).

At the end of each chapter are BrainWork activities—mental exercises related to the subject of the chapter. These exercises don't have right or wrong answers—they are designed to get you thinking in new ways.

When you come upon the BrainWork symbol in the text, go to the end of the chapter and complete that particular BrainWork exercise. When you've completed the exercise, go back to the text and keep reading.

Once you've completed a chapter, turn to the back of the book to read some reflections on the chapter's BrainWork exercises. Don't use the back of the book to figure out how many answers you got right. Instead think about your responses in light of the end-of-the-book reflections, and see what insights you gain.

At first, some BrainWork questions may seem strange and difficult. That is intentional. Each question is meant to require you to think differently. As you work through each BrainWork, remember that *Positive Attitude Development* comes only through daily repetition of powerful mental exercises.

In fact, we encourage you to use the BrainWork exercises over and over as you practice and keep building your Positive Attitude Development.

We hope you enjoy your adventure.

I began to picture an attitude as the cloud from which our thoughts rain.
Next, I imagined thoughts nourishing the soil from which our actions grow.
And finally, I saw our actions blossoming into a positive, meaningful life.

Introduction

After six months in the Milan, Michigan, federal prison, my daily pulse rate was 101 beats per minute and I couldn't get it to slow down. One day, as my table started to shake, I was convinced there'd been a nearly impossible event: a Magnitude Six earthquake in Michigan.

I felt I was falling out of my chair and lunged across the aisle to stabilize myself. Before my hand reached the other side, an inmate grabbed my arm and said, "Hey dude, you better do something or you're never going to make it out of prison alive." At that moment, I realized I was in trouble and something had to give.

Back then, I was convinced that everything in my life would be okay if things outside me (like other people and events) changed. If other people did what I thought they should do, then my stress would dissipate, peace would descend—and so would my heart rate. I was furious because those external stressors weren't changing (or staying the same) the way I wanted.

The situation seemed much worse because I was locked behind a prison fence with no

way to influence the outside world—and I was convinced that the external world was causing all my pain. Everything just kept getting worse, and I was in serious trouble because it seemed like there was nothing I could do to change the situation. If none of the events and people on the outside were going to change (in spite of my expectations, desires and demands), there was no way to reduce my stress and possibly save my life!

I was at risk of dying for no medical reason. But what could I do? I was imprisoned by the government and by my own stress, anger and anxiety.

Of course, many other inmates were stressing out too. But I noticed some old timers who looked very calm. They seemed capable of dealing with losing everything they were attached to—including control of their daily activities and any ability to influence outside people and events.

I started asking the old timers, "What do you know that I don't?" They simply said, "You just have to put your life on hold until you get out and then pick up whatever pieces are left." That sounded right, but it still didn't relieve the pain of seeing everything I was attached to falling away. I was frozen in the moment of my arrest for drug dealing, while everyone else in my life was moving onward.

It was at this point of my incarceration that a fellow prisoner, Dan L. Bayes, asked me to co-facilitate a positive attitude class that aimed to teach other inmates how to deal with change. While wondering what I could offer anyone about accepting change, this opportunity drove me to study the connection between change and attitude. The experience eventually gave me a new lease on life, ultimately helping me to feel free—even as I spent 18 more years behind bars. I realized the process for accepting change begins with one's attitude. As I enriched my own attitude I began to see everything, including my relationships, differently. This was huge!

For more than 18 years, in cooperation with prison staff, I've taught this Positive Attitude Development course in federal prisons at three security levels, each course running 20 weeks or more. The programs have been well received by inmates, with some taking the course multiple times.

For those of us who adopted PAD, life was no longer a battle that we had to fight every day. Even while we were restricted by incarceration, our lives became a journey. Instead of waiting for release to pick up the pieces, we began building a new life on the inside. This was the most freeing experience of my life. I now had control over how I felt about everything. My happiness was not based on the way events happened (whether within the prison or "on the outside"), but rather on the way I interpreted those events.

I began to picture an attitude as the cloud from which our thoughts rain. Next, I imagined thoughts nourishing the soil from which our actions grow. And finally, I saw our actions blossoming into a positive, meaningful life.

The texture and quality of our attitude determines the type of life we build for ourselves. That's the foundation of Positive Attitude Development, which can offer the beginning of a new life for each of us—no matter what our circumstances.

I know that inmates are not the only people who feel trapped by circumstances. If you have ever felt "imprisoned" by people, places or situations in your life, then this book has answers that can work for you—because they've worked in the extreme environment of prisons.

Lyle, your Positive Attitude Development *course helped change my life. It taught me how to recognize my core values, how to look for the good in people and things, and how to see that my happiness does not depend on how people treat me—but on how I treat other people. This course was one of the most eye-opening, uplifting times in my life! Thank you so very much.*

Your friend forever,
John Gelnette, former federal prisoner

Awareness

POSITIVE ATTITUDE DEVELOPMENT

ATTITUDE

There is hope.

I can change.

It's up to me.

Your brain is the hardware of your soul. It is the hardware of your very essence as a human being. You cannot be who you really want to be unless your brain works right. How your brain works determines how happy you are, how effective you feel, and how well you interact with others.

—Daniel G. Amen, M.D.
Change Your Brain, Change Your Life

In this session:

- The power of our thoughts
- How beliefs can hijack our thoughts
- The role of beliefs

Feel Free to Change Your Mind: Brain Awareness

THE POSITIVE ATTITUDE DEVELOPMENT (PAD) program is based on the belief that the brain—a changeable organ—produces our behavior. To change our behavior, we need neurological reconstruction. We can think of it as remodeling our brains.

Our brain develops its own unique neurological networks, influenced by our unique daily experiences that trigger or inhibit our propensities. In a sense, during our time in uterus, our DNA creates a brain ready to be programmed. Our experiences help program our neural networks as we grow through life. Our brains in turn adjust

Some Rules for Unhappiness

First, you must make sure that all the little, insignificant things in life bother you. Don't just leave it to chance. Sit down and get worked up over things that really don't matter.

Next, make sure that you lose your perspective on things. At all costs, make mountains out of molehills and make crises out of the regular happenings of everyday life.

When you're done with that, get yourself in a state of worry. Make sure when you pick something to worry about, you choose something you can do absolutely nothing about. This will ensure your failure and cost you a lot of time you can't afford—and then you can worry about that, too.

When you're ready, launch out into the world of perfectionism. Condemn yourself and others for not being able to achieve an unachievable goal. When you make a mistake, rail against yourself.

After you have mastered perfectionism, you will then be ready to be right all the time.
Be rigid in your rightness. Never allow for anyone else's perspectives.

The next step: never trust anyone and never believe in anyone. Look for everyone's weakness, and concentrate on that. Always think poorly of yourself, too. Never think that you are good enough for anyone or anything.

Anything that happens to you must be taken personally at all times.

And finally, never totally give yourself to anyone or anything.

and adapt to help us address and/or survive our life experiences.

Recent research shows that we can construct new neurological pathways in our brains to improve our attitudes and our lives. But successful reconstruction requires us to block off the old, problematic neural activity at the same time that we create new pathways that produce our desired habits and behaviors. The old problematic pathways are well-worn and comforting in their familiarity, but they lead to negative consequences. So it takes sustained, conscious effort to go down the new, less-traveled path (especially if people around us remain on the old trail). In other words, our brains are still susceptible to defaulting to old behavior if the reconstruction is not maintained.

To change behavior we have to change the workings of our brains—to change the processing system originally developed in response to our life experiences. With practice, we can have our brains prune unused dendrites (the parts of nerve cells that produce impulses) and delete those parts that reinforced our old negative behavior. We can also reinforce its new neural activity to support the behavior we want and need.

The Positive Attitude Development program (PAD) facilitates this process for personal change. It was developed by inmates serving long prison terms in medium-, low- and minimum-security federal prisons and has been adapted for use by the general non-prison public. PAD begins by raising awareness of the brain's immense power, using examples of how our brains respond when we're confronted by sudden change. We'll study this phenomenon for a simple reason: The way the brain habitually assimilates, accommodates, and acclimates to change determines the quality of life—and can even determine its longevity.

BrainWork indicates activity sheets that follow each chapter.

BrainWork: 10-Year Peace-to-Chaos Continuum

BrainWork: Beliefs

BrainWork: Choices

PAD will help us become aware of the attitude (and its supporting beliefs) that distorts our thinking and our perception of our actual circumstances.

Summary

This lesson increases awareness of powerful thought patterns. Responding to sudden change with negative patterns of thought generates negative behaviors and outcomes. But the power of a positive thought pattern can give us hope to create better attitude and a positive future. We need to be aware that if we change our attitude, we can change our life.

The process of changing our future through Positive Attitude Development:

Adopting new beliefs,
which lead to

Better attitudes,
which lead to

Healthier thoughts,
which lead to

New actions,
which lead to

Different habits,
which lead to

Character,
which leads to

A new destiny.

How do we develop our attitude? That's what we'll be talking about the rest of our time together.

BrainWork

10-Year Peace-to-Chaos Continuum

We all live our days somewhere along a continuum between feeling that life is peaceful or chaotic. Circle one of the numbers below to indicate where you were on this continuum 10 years ago. Then draw an arrow to show the direction you were headed back then.

10 years ago, where were you on this continuum,
and in what direction were you headed?

10 years ago

1   2   3   4   5   6   7   8   9   10

PEACE <--> CHAOS

Today, where are you on this continuum, and in what direction are you headed?

Today

1   2   3   4   5   6   7   8   9   10

PEACE <--> CHAOS

BrainWork

Beliefs

Beliefs play a big role in our lives, but we're not always clear about what we think about our beliefs or core values. Write down your thoughts about the questions below. Use another sheet of paper if you need it. After you're done, take a look at page 79 to see some of our thoughts on the subject.

How do you believe a person's attitude relates (if at all) to a person's fate?

_____

_____

_____

_____

_____

How do you believe that what people say to themselves—the thoughts they express—relate to their fate?

_____

_____

_____

_____

_____

What are some of your beliefs and thoughts about your current life situation?

_____

_____

_____

_____

Beliefs *continued*

List three positive ways you could use the power of your thoughts.

1. _____

2. _____

3. _____

Connect all nine of these dots by using only 4 straight lines, without lifting your pen from the page.

Answer, page 80

BrainWork

Choices

Our beliefs, attitudes and thoughts have a direct impact on the choices we make. Answer these questions honestly, and try answering them without blaming anyone else for the choices you're describing. See page 80 for our thoughts about these issues.

Describe a time when your past negative attitude and thought process influenced your choices.

_____

_____

_____

_____

_____

What beliefs hijacked your thoughts in that situation?

_____

_____

_____

_____

_____

List some different beliefs that might have brought about better results for you.

_____

_____

_____

_____

_____

Choices *continued*

Fill in these circles with one to five words that describe some beliefs that hijack your thoughts today. Examples of things other people have written are "everyone is out to get me" and "I'm stupid." See page 81 for our thoughts about these issues.

Beliefs

Choices *continued*

See page 82 for our thoughts about these issues.

Is your destiny the result of your past thoughts?

_____
_____
_____
_____
_____

Why do some people see the glass half full, and others see it as half empty?

_____
_____
_____
_____
_____
_____

What is an attitude?

_____
_____
_____
_____
_____

Thinking

POSITIVE ATTITUDE DEVELOPMENT

◆ **ATTITUDE** ◆

I can choose.

Thoughts create behavior.

I can arrest negative thinking.

In this session:

- The thought shift
- Baseline attitude
- Mental diet
- Resistance to change
- Forgive and forget?

Our cells are constantly eavesdropping on our thoughts and being changed by them. A bout of depression can wreak havoc with the immune system; falling in love can boost it. Despair and hopelessness raise the risk of heart attacks and cancer, thereby shortening life. Joy and fulfillment keep us healthy and extend life. This means that the line between biology and psychology can't really be drawn with any certainty. A remembered stress, which is only a wisp of thought, releases the same flood of destructive hormones as the stress itself.

—Deepak Chropra, M.D.
Ageless Body, Timeless Mind

Warning! Contagious! The Power of Thinking

DURING THE YEARS I TAUGHT Positive Attitude Development in prisons, people often told me that to change my destiny, I simply had to change my thinking. But the experience of teaching PAD to thousands of inmates showed me that the dynamic is more complex. If I simply try to have positive thoughts, but those thoughts are inconsistent with my existing core values, then I'll default back to my old thinking pattern—the same pattern

God, grant me the serenity to accept the persons I cannot change,

The courage to change the person I can, and

The wisdom to know it's me.

—William C. Klatte

What you live with, you learn.

What you learn, you practice.

What you practice, you become.

What you become has consequences.

—Earnie Larsen

When I came to prison, I began a new life. I had to become master of my emotions because I could no longer go around out of control like I had most of my life. I was filled with hatred, envy, and strife; jealous of anyone who had the good life. Since I have been [in prison], I have learned to greet each day with love in my heart. Love can overcome anything.

As I look around [this prison], I see faces of self-confidence; faces of satisfaction from taking this Positive Attitude Development class. I see faces laughing at the world with high esteem, because in spite of our situation, we will persist until we succeed.

—Federal prisoner, Elkton, Ohio

that landed me in prison. We may try to keep good thoughts, but if we don't train the brain to maintain a positive attitude, then (especially at life's crucial, high-stress moments), we default to our old destructive pathways of thinking—and that makes failure our reward.

Some neurologists suggest that humans have a baseline attitude, formed during the prenatal period when billions of neural connections are made. For millions of years, the human brain has slowly evolved to help us survive and thrive in a slowly changing human environment. But over the past century, the rate of social, technological and other change in our human environment has reached breathtaking speed—a speed that continues to accelerate. The rapidly changing environment in which we currently live is different from the environment in which the brain originally emerged. So it's no surprise that we regularly feel confusion and chaos in our lives—even if we've never been in jail.

This might sound as if we're condemned to discord and unhappiness. Fortunately, current research into the brain also reveals an important, refreshing reality: the brain has plasticity, which makes it possible for it to reshape itself for survival and enjoyment of life. We truly can develop our attitude because the brain is changeable—it's not locked into a static neurological landscape, preventing the possibility of a new and better life.

Because of the brain's plasticity, it can be re-formed. This is a profound concept. But we must also remember that change can go both ways; in order for us to become new people, our minds must police themselves and arrest the return of destructive thoughts we developed earlier in life.

The first requirement is changing the present mode of thinking. We have to put our brain on a mental diet, replacing junk thoughts with balanced, healthy ones. This requires that the mind be clear, tenacious and efficient in inhibiting its past negative activity, replacing the old thoughts with new and desirable ones. Negative thoughts are contagious, so we have to stand guard over our new thoughts to protect our future.

The consequences of a prisoner's old thoughts are easy to see—for example, incarceration! But people who've never been to jail also have negative thoughts and beliefs which produce unpleasant consequences like addiction, divorce and anxiety. Given those stakes, it's important to realize that a single negative thought never stands alone in the human brain; it is supported by other negative thoughts, and working together, they generate negative behaviors. If we aren't vigilant, our old thoughts will remain within, attract other negative thoughts and degrade our quality of life.

The stakes are high—but so are the rewards. Let's start by examining the thoughts and action that produced your present situation—even if it is something less dire than imprisonment. We'll carefully examine our past actions, but then we'll take a further, important step. We'll ask what supporting thoughts helped create our past actions and begin to understand how our brains work. When we uncover the supporting thoughts, we'll seek out the beliefs that supported them. Once we discover those beliefs, we'll be at the threshold of developing an enduring positive attitude. This effort requires a tenacity and efficiency at this juncture in our lives that can change the possibilities for our futures and offer us a new and exciting life. Now let's turn to our discussion and see what we can discover together about ourselves.

BrainWork: Example: Auto-Pilot Thinking

BrainWork: Your Thoughts on Automatic Pilot

The difficulty of change

Clasp your hands together with your fingers folded over each other in a natural manner. Does this feel normal or comfortable? Now shift the fingers on your right hand over one spot. Does this feel normal or comfortable?

The brain wants you to keep it (and thus you) in its default position. It works for your comfort, but not necessarily for your success—unless you change its default patterns. Changing your brain's default patterns requires putting it on a new mental diet.

BrainWork : What Are You Thinking?

Summary

This lesson teaches the process for Positive Attitude Development. It challenges our default thinking by questioning some of our basic beliefs and asking how they have contributed to our present situation.

Example: Auto-Pilot Thinking

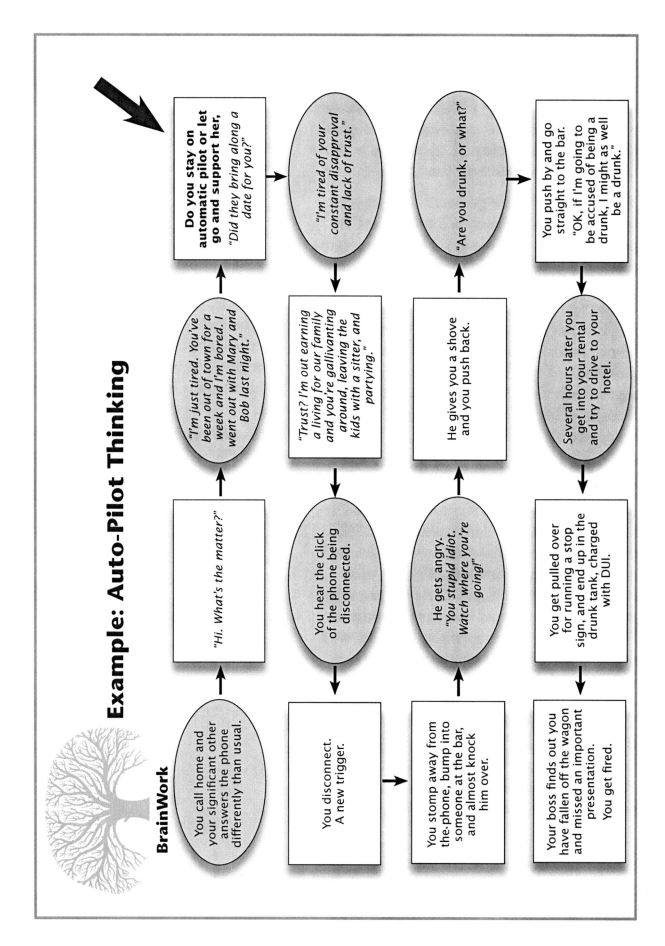

BrainWork

You call home and your significant other answers the phone differently than usual.

"Hi. What's the matter?"

"I'm just tired. You've been out of town for a week and I'm bored. I went out with Mary and Bob last night."

Do you stay on automatic pilot or let go and support her, "Did they bring along a date for you?"

"I'm tired of your constant disapproval and lack of trust."

"Trust? I'm out earning a living for our family and you're gallivanting around, leaving the kids with a sitter, and partying."

You hear the click of the phone being disconnected.

You disconnect. A new trigger.

You stomp away from the phone, bump into someone at the bar, and almost knock him over.

He gets angry. "You stupid idiot. Watch where you're going!"

He gives you a shove and you push back.

"Are you drunk, or what?"

You push by and go straight to the bar. "OK, if I'm going to be accused of being a drunk, I might as well be a drunk."

Several hours later you get into your rental and try to drive to your hotel.

You get pulled over for running a stop sign, and end up in the drunk tank, charged with DUI.

Your boss finds out you have fallen off the wagon and missed an important presentation. You get fired.

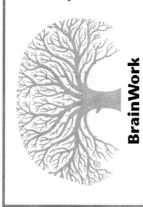

BrainWork

Your Thoughts on Automatic Pilot

Use this space to describe a situation in your own life like the one demonstrated on p. 22. Draw boxes to illustrate what you said, thought and did; and draw ovals for what other people said or did.

23

BrainWork

What Are *You* Thinking?

Write down your thoughts about the questions below. Use another sheet of paper if you need it. After you're done, take a look at page 82 to see some of our thoughts on the subject.

Those who cannot remember the past are condemned to repeat it. —**George Santayana**

What's the first thought that comes to mind when you see each of these words?

Anger _____

Sex _____

Betrayal _____

Joy _____

Love _____

Forgiveness _____

What do you think it means to begin a new life?

_____

How can you begin a new life in your current circumstances?

_____

Do you need to forget the past to begin a new life?

_____

How important is forgiveness in beginning a new life?

_____

Are there any actions that you just can't forgive? If so, what are they?

_____

What purpose does it serve to bury the hatchet if you're going to mark the spot?

_____

If we do not learn from the past, are we condemned to repeat it?

_____

Trust

POSITIVE ATTITUDE DEVELOPMENT

In this session:

- Conceive, believe, achieve
- SNIOP/SPIOP
- Contagious thoughts
- Repelling thoughts
- The bed vs. the train

ATTITUDE

I can change my thoughts.

Thoughts are contagious.

My mind influences my body.

Trust That It Works

THE MOST IMPORTANT ELEMENT for change is learning to trust the universe. Why trust the universe? Because it's pretty reliable. If we heat water (to 212° Fahrenheit or 100° Celsius at sea level), it will boil and turn into steam. If we cool it down (to 32° Fahrenheit or 0° Celsius at sea level), it will freeze. We can boil or freeze H_2O over and over again for the rest of our lives, and we'll always get the same result. The same holds true for millions of other chemical, physical and biological reactions that we can rely on in the animal, plant and mineral worlds.

Likewise, if you take the same actions over and over again, in the same or similar situations, it is extremely likely that you will get the same result. If you get angry and call your spouse or partner a nasty name, the odds are high that she or he will be upset in response.

Do it a third time and what happens?

We have to trust that, in our universe, like attitudes produce like thoughts and vice versa. A negative attitude tends to produce negative thoughts and negative thoughts tend to produce

My name is Kim. My story begins when I was released from prison. Before I got out, I completed a drug and alcohol program and was making a fresh, new start in life. I started by hanging out on the beach enjoying the sun and people and feeling alive and free, taking time for myself, something I'd never done before. After getting a job at the concession stand on the beach, I was in heaven, making a few bucks and being on the beach daily. Then with summer almost over, I knew I needed to find another job. I found work at a janitorial service, making $6.25 an hour. Not much, but a job all the same. I put my best work forward and it paid off.

After a few weeks of cleaning bathrooms and offices, I was offered a job building houses. But when I tried to resign from the janitorial company, they said they liked my work and couldn't let me go. Instead, they made me a manager in charge of 40 employees at 13 separate buildings, taking care of many details, dealing with customer complaints, ordering supplies, etc., etc. Being a boss was something I didn't expect in my future, having just left prison as a convicted felon. It just goes to show, keep your head up, push forward, and good things will happen.

I was a good boss. I used your positive attitude approach with my employees and customers. Our monthly complaint rate fell from between 40 and 60 to just a few. I did this by personally speaking to the people and directing solutions to their complaints in person, then following through by talking to the employee responsible and checking later to

negative attitudes—which in turn produce negative actions and negative consequences. This is a basic idea that may be simplistic, but it's nevertheless true.

I'm asking you to trust that PAD is a process that will develop healthy thoughts, beliefs, attitude and actions. If you're tenacious and courageous about PAD, you'll begin to experience the wonders and mysteries of life—catching your imagination and spirit and filling your life with fun and excitement.

Do you believe that what the mind can conceive and believe, it can achieve? I do, because I've seen remarkable evidence of it.

Take former insurance executive Morris Goodman, whom I met when he spoke to PAD participants in our prison. In 1981, Morris crashed his single-engine aircraft, breaking vertebrae, damaging his spinal cord. He was left paralyzed from the neck down. By the time rescuers brought Morris to the hospital, physicians were amazed he was still alive. The only way he could communicate was by blinking his eyes once for "yes" and twice for "no."

Before emergency surgery, doctors told Morris that his chances for survival were slim. Afterward, he still couldn't move, breathe, or eat on his own. But, Morris explains, "After I lived through the surgery, I set a goal to walk out of the hospital in six months. My sister made a chart of letters to help me communicate. To make myself understood to the outside world, my sister and I developed a system of blinks that indicated the letter I wanted, and through this very slow process, I put together words and sentences to express my thoughts and decisions. Nothing was going to stop me from recovering."

He overcame astounding odds in the process. For example, the injuries left Morris' diaphragm muscle unable to expand and contract his lungs—

he had to be tethered to a breathing machine. So, he set out to teach himself how to use his still-working stomach muscles to do the job instead. He mastered this seemingly impossible feat and succeeded in breathing without any machines.

Morris had to relearn how to swallow, speak and perform many other basic bodily functions. Doctors and other professionals told him that such a complete recovery was impossible. Morris responded by asking, "Why?" When they said they'd never seen anyone do it before, Morris decided to set his goals higher than what others saw for him or expected from him.

When Morris met with us in prison, he was adamant that it took more than determination and hard work to recover. Crucial to his recovery was visualization: seeing himself totally recovered—and not settling for "just walking out of the hospital."

His method wasn't easy: Morris explains that it required putting his mind on a strict mental diet of only positive beliefs, thoughts and attitudes. It also meant finding and bringing together people (like his sister) who believed as he did—that the cells of his body were eavesdropping on the positive, recovery-focused thoughts of his mind—and responding accordingly.

This last part of Morris' method helps illustrate the important principles of "SNIOP" and "SPIOP." As humans, we are Susceptible to the Negative Influences of Other People (SNIOP). You'd be right to think that prison is one of the best places to observe SNIOP. After all, bad decisions land most felons in the joint, where all that negativity easily feeds on itself.

But our experience with PAD in prison also shows how much we humans are also Susceptible to the Positive Influences of Other People (SPIOP). Key

make sure the area was cleaned properly.

After 13 months of continuous service, never missing a day of work, my job was eliminated, with the company claiming I hadn't disclosed my complete felony record at the time of hiring. I'd given the H.R. department a complete copy of my record from the courthouse and talked about the nature of my felonies with the person hiring me. In the end it didn't make any difference. I was fired. I started collecting unemployment and looking for a new job.

I have a wonderful woman in my life. With her encouragement and love, I pushed on.

After close to three months of not finding a job (and not trying too hard to find one), I found construction work. The men on the crew were typical construction types, all drinkers. Coming from a long history of dysfunctional drinking myself, I did what I said I'd never do again. After a ten-hour day one Friday, we all stopped at a bar. I thought, "I'm one of the men and I can handle this." After most of the guys left, I was still there with my boss talking shop and getting drunk. It was around 1:00 a.m. when I got into my truck to make my way home. I was pulled over, resulting in my sixth drunk driving offense. My life, my woman, my kids and my positive attitude were put on hold. As a result, I'm at Gordon Correctional Center in Wisconsin.

I hope this helps others to see that the problem is always there and that even the strong fall. I'm picking up the pieces once again. I'd love to start building that positive, untouchable feeling again—and then share it with others here at Gordon.

—Kim Modrow

Other people call you Nicotine, but we've been together all these years, so I'm going to call you Nicky. I've come to realize that you've misled me for so long about what you are to me and what you can do for me.

You remind me a lot of some relationships I've had before with other people—where I thought only of what they were like in the beginning: all the love, the good times, how we did everything together, and how hard it was to continue without that person. In the past, when I wanted to let you go (much like my relationships with people), you would manipulate me and say, "Let's talk about this tomorrow." But I've put this off so long already.

The truth is, Nicky; my relationship with you is killing me. You sure aren't my friend because friends don't leave you coughing or make you unable to breathe. When I sleep at night, I hear what you've done to my lungs—the wheezing. You cause me nothing but harm and unhappiness and unless I end this relationship with you, you'll cause my death.

I know I'll have a period in my life that I may even grieve over not having you, but that will pass. It will go away and I'll see that I'm so very, very much better off without you. Good-bye, Nicky; don't come back. I don't need you anymore

— **Stewert Van Maasdam**
Duluth Federal Prison Camp

to the success of PAD in prison (as in any other environment—including your own) is to actively find support from other like-minded people. And, from what we've learned so far about the brain, I mean like-minded quite literally.

Take my friend Stu whose story you read on the left. He was a lifelong smoker stuck in prison. After his PAD training, fellow participants supported Stewert as he took the major step of breaking free of his nicotine addiction by changing his beliefs, thoughts and attitudes about the problem.

BrainWork: Susceptibility Scan

BrainWork: Beliefs, Thoughts, and Actions

Summary

This lesson shows the power of a tenaciously positive attitude—even when confronted with sudden, extreme change. It reveals the concrete connection between our thoughts and our physical lives.

BrainWork

Susceptibility Scan

Write down your thoughts about the questions below. Use another sheet of paper if you need it. After you have completed it, take a look at page 84 to see some of our thoughts on the subject.

Write out the words associated with the letters below.

S _____   S _____

N _____   P _____

I _____   I _____

O _____   O _____

P _____   P _____

How did Morris Goodman repel SNIOP in his recovery?

_____

_____

Morris put himself on a strict mental diet—but it wasn't a diet of deprivation, like a weight-loss program uses. What kind of nourishment did Morris feed his brain while on his mental diet?

_____

_____

Give some examples of negative influences you have to overcome in your life.

_____

_____

What negative influences, if any, will you experience in the future?

_____

_____

BrainWork

Beliefs, Thoughts, and Actions

Write down your thoughts about the questions below. Use another sheet of paper if you need it. After you've completed your answers, take a look at page 85 to see some of our thoughts on the subject.

What do you think would have happened to you if you had been in an accident like Morris Goodman had?

_____

_____

What would your beliefs, thoughts and attitudes have been in that situation?

_____

_____

What is the difference between those beliefs, thoughts and attitudes and the ones that Morris seems to have in his recovery?

_____

_____

Put these differences into these three categories:

Beliefs	Thoughts	Actions
Success is beyond my reach.	_There is no need to try. I can't do it._	_I do all the things to make my belief come true._

In the Moment

POSITIVE ATTITUDE DEVELOPMENT

ATTITUDE

I can't live tomorrow until it's here.
There is no better yesterday.
Now is all I have.

In this session:

- 60,000 thoughts a day
- Build a better yesterday
- Eternal moments
- Illusion of control

The Seven-Second Life

MANY AREAS OF A PRISONER'S LIFE are managed by others (like the prison staff), without the inmate's permission or input. However, hundreds of PAD-trained prisoners have shown that, despite our incarceration, important portions of our lives—especially our thoughts—remain to be managed by us.

The same thing holds true for you, too. For example, some 60,000 thoughts pass through our brains every day—thoughts that aren't controlled by anyone outside of ourselves.

Think about how many things a prison guard can order an inmate to do every day. Five? Twenty-five? Even 100 demands are puny compared to the 60,000 thoughts we can control each day. That's great news! Nevertheless, our thoughts are often negative ones, like thoughts bemoaning the way our lives are managed by outside circumstances— even if we've never been near a prison. If we really can control our thoughts, why would so many of them be negative? It's because of the way we visualize our situation.

When Mark Twain was an old man, a reporter asked him: "How do you remain calm and reassured in the declining years of your life?"

Twain answered: "I select two days of each week to be free of worry."

"Oh," replied the reporter. "That's an interesting strategy. Which two days do you chose?"

Twain answered, "Yesterday and tomorrow."

The thoughts we have every 24 hours (on average, one thought every 1.44 seconds) constitute a strongly rushing stream. That stream is our core of life that we can and must begin to manage more effectively.

To live fully, we have to narrow our attention to a controllable span of experience and time, aka the present. The secret is to understand that we will never have a better past. The past is what it is and that's not going to change. The only thing about the past that can change is the way that we see and use past experiences in our lives today. We can change the attitudes and behaviors that produced our past actions and their consequences.

To live fully in the present moment requires that we don't live in the future, either. We have to avoid imagining the future in ways that destroy our window of life or daily portal of experience. We can prepare for the future, but we can't live tomorrow until it's here. If we try to, we miss the present.

Here's the bottom line: We can't change the past or the future; the universe doesn't allow it. Trying to change the past or the future is a waste of our time and energy— just like we'd be wasting our time and energy trying to get water to boil or freeze

at 85°. No amount of effort is going to make it happen.

We'll begin learning how to live in the moment by zooming in on a few drops of our gushing, often turbulent, stream of thoughts: those drops of thought we're having during a seven-second window of our own experience.

BrainWork: Zeroing in on Now

BrainWork: Fear Factors

Homework: Use **BrainWork: Zeroing in on Now** three times a day, every day until the next session.

Summary

This lesson shows the importance of shrinking our attention to seven seconds: two seconds that are fading, the three we are in, and the two that are approaching. This moment of eternity is where we can fully live. This lesson shows how to participate in this moment of eternity and enjoy life as it comes.

BrainWork

Zeroing in on Now

What is your present stream of thought?

Time yourself for 10 seconds and quickly jot down words, images or other keys that reflect the conscious thoughts you have during that 10-second period.

Use the spaces below to repeat the exercise in a few minutes, later in the day, and in the future. Use another sheet of paper and repeat the activity every day until we meet again.

See page 86 for our thoughts on these issues.

Eternity

Birth **Now-7 Seconds** *Death*

Eternity

Speed Write-Down 1

_____ _____ _____

_____ _____ _____

_____ _____ _____

Speed Write-Down 2

_____ _____ _____

_____ _____ _____

_____ _____ _____

Speed Write-Down 3

_____ _____ _____

_____ _____ _____

_____ _____ _____

BrainWork

Fear Factors

Write down your thoughts about the questions below. When you have completed your answers, look on page 87 for our thoughts about these issues.

The biggest killers of time are: Procrastination, Doubt, and Fear. Fear can be defined as False Evidence Appearing Real or Fantasized Experiences Appearing Real.

How do you define fear?

F _____

E _____

A _____

R _____

Describe a time when false or fantasized experiences appeared real in your life.

_____

_____

If you knew you were going to die tonight, what would you do with the rest of today?

_____

_____

_____

Now, think about the legacy you want to leave your loved ones. If you knew you were going to die tonight, what would you do with the rest of today?

_____

_____

_____

POSITIVE ATTITUDE DEVELOPMENT

Tenacity

ATTITUDE

I can succeed.

I can accomplish.

I can live smart.

In this session:

- Is failure genetic?
- Persistence!
- What we've sacrificed
- Vocabulary diet
- Smart living

Talking Tenacity: The Power of Persistence

IS FAILURE GENETIC, or are people conditioned to fail? There's no evidence that failure is wired into our DNA, our blood, our heritage, or our biological makeup. After more than two decades in prison, I know countless stories of men who were conditioned to fail, expected to fail, and frequently resisted taking even the simplest steps toward success.

One example is a former gang member, my friend and fellow inmate Shane. By the time Shane got to prison, he expected to fail in life. When he faced failure, he didn't go to others for help, because he believed the world had either turned against him or given up on him. Shane was convinced that nobody was interested in helping him.

But after working on positive attitude development, he began trying tenacity and trusting that he could succeed. For example, Shane decided to conscientiously complete all of the tasks expected by the parole board. He doggedly

35

O.K. So I lost my Wonder-Bread job. Did I let that stop me or slow me down? Hell NO! I was looking for a job when I got that one! So I hit the bricks (in my car, of course) and found a job as a plumber for $10.00 an hour with all the bennies. And I like my job. The owner said I impressed her with my honesty by laying everything out on the table. I was in prison for 14 years. It was a dope charge. I knew nothing about plumbing.

But on the other hand, I'm a hard worker. I show up on time. I went to college while in prison. I was part of the Youth Awareness Program. I taught recovery and relapse classes for over three years. I attended PAD classes for over 60 weeks. And on and on.

So anyway, I got the job and I like the job.

—Monte Apfel

followed their recommendations, anticipating that this would lead directly to the shortening of his sentence.

But after repeated appearances before the board, Shane still wasn't paroled. He was denied because the parole board could find no record of Shane completing one of his required classes. Shane always assured them that he'd taken it, but the board didn't budge. He left these hearings frustrated and angry at the world.

The next time Shane was eligible to go before the parole board, his frustration hadn't dissipated. He told the prison staff, "Why bother going back there? I do what they tell me to do, and it doesn't make any difference—they don't believe me. The 90-minute trip will be a waste of my time, your time and the gas."

Despite Shane's objection, his case manager signed him up for an appointment anyway. So Shane once again told the parole board that he'd followed all of their instructions. But the board still couldn't find a record of Shane completing that one certain class.

Shane felt his frustration bubbling over again. He looked over at the staff from his prison. They knew he'd completed the class, but they weren't doing anything. So Shane nudged one of them and said, "Isn't there any way you can look this up somewhere and show them that I took the class?"

At that, one of the staffers went over to a nearby computer. Within ten minutes, she found the official document proving Shane's completion of the class, printed it out, and handed it over to the parole board. The parole board promptly cut the final year from Shane's sentence, and he was released less than two weeks later.

Even though Shane hadn't fully realized it then, he'd begun to cast aside his old beliefs that people were out to get him, the world had no use for him, and no one would help him.

Despite being very angry and frustrated in the moment, Shane had asked for help. Help was there—and he won a year of freedom just by showing tenacity for ten minutes longer than he'd planned.

When a setback (like losing a job) happens, it may feel like an insurmountable failure. At such times, we have a couple of choices: "giving up" to stay where we are, or "giving up" to move on. Throwing up our hands in despair keeps us in a cycle of failure, being weak and feeling worthless. The stronger, healthier option is to adopt a different course: letting go of setbacks and accepting them as temporary, rather than dwelling on them as if they are permanent. In fact, something that appears to be failure is often a step along the road to success.

Hall-of-Famer Barry Sanders (1989–1998) has the third most rushing yards in NFL history. Sanders also holds the NFL record for the most carries for negative yardage (according to *Sports Illustrated: The Football Book*, it's 336 carries for losses of 952 yards). But lost yardage was central to what made Sanders' running style so electric and effective. His Detroit Lions team was usually weak; when he ran into resistance at the line, he reversed field—often retreating 10 to 20 yards in order to gain 5 or 10—or a whole lot more.

Reggie Jackson has the most career postseason home runs: 18. He's Top 10 for career homers in the pre-steroid era (563). He also has the most strikeouts in a career: 2,597. Averaging about 500 at-bats a season over 21 years, Jackson spent five full seasons striking out, and a little more than one season hitting homers. Which statistic is Jackson remembered for?

BrainWork: A Vocabulary Diet

BrainWork: Determining Your Success

BrainWork: Through Valleys to Peaks

BrainWork: Tracking Your Personal Development

Summary

This lesson shows the importance of persistence, because both failure and success are inevitable parts of life. It shows ways to repel negative attitude, beliefs and thoughts so that we can reach our goals.

BrainWork

A Vocabulary Diet

Write down your thoughts about the questions below. Use another sheet of paper if you need it. After you've completed your answers, see page 87 to see some of our thoughts on the subject.

How are you tested or challenged every day?

_____

_____

Certain words or phrases promote failure. What words or phrases have you heard other people use that you think have promoted failure in their lives?

_____

_____

What words or phrases have you used that you think have promoted failure in your life?

_____

_____

What things do you tell yourself that erode your motivation?

_____

_____

What words or phrases do you need to remove from your vocabulary to help you reach your goals?

_____

_____

Which of these statements do you believe?

A. Failure is genetic.   B. We become conditioned to fail.

BrainWork

Determining Your Success

Write down your thoughts about the questions below. Use another sheet of paper if you need it. After you've completed your answers, see page 88 to see some of our thoughts on the subject.

What have you given up on in the past that, upon reflection, you know you could have accomplished if you'd persisted?

_____

_____

What are some small steps you've taken to reach a goal?

_____

_____

What's a positive way to perceive obstacles and adversity?

_____

_____

Is life like the Super Bowl—does your winning depend on someone else losing?

_____

_____

What other ways might there be to perceive success?

_____

_____

BrainWork

Through Valleys to Peaks

Ohio State Head Football Coach Jim Tressel says that life's low points are necessary; it's in the lows, when you face obstacles, that you get what you need to go higher. Coach Tressel came to the federal prison in Elkton, Ohio, and explained how a player develops— or fails to develop—over four years.

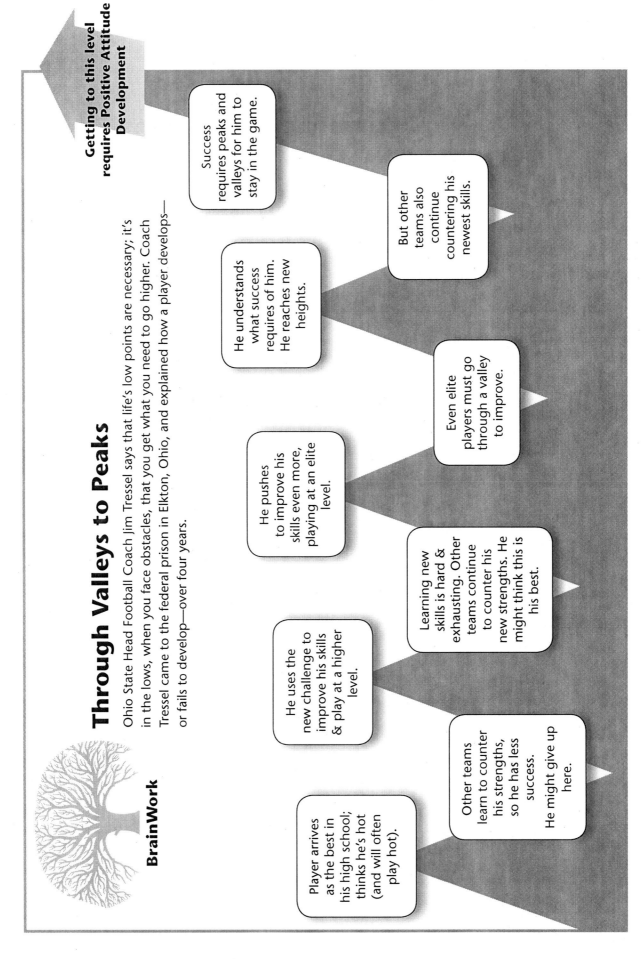

Getting to this level requires Positive Attitude Development

Success requires peaks and valleys for him to stay in the game.

But other teams also continue countering his newest skills.

He understands what success requires of him. He reaches new heights.

Even elite players must go through a valley to improve.

He pushes to improve his skills even more, playing at an elite level.

Learning new skills is hard & exhausting. Other teams continue to counter his new strengths. He might think this is his best.

He uses the new challenge to improve his skills & play at a higher level.

Other teams learn to counter his strengths, so he has less success.

He might give up here.

Player arrives as the best in his high school; thinks he's hot (and will often play hot).

BrainWork

Tracking Your Personal Development

See page 89 for our thoughts about these issues.

What are some examples of what you've learned in some of the peaks and valleys of your life?

Peaks

_____

_____

_____

_____

_____

_____

Valleys

_____

_____

_____

_____

_____

_____

_____

_____

If we never screw up, we never learn life's most important lessons.
Remember to honor your mistakes.

—Joe Kelly

POSITIVE ATTITUDE DEVELOPMENT

Umbrella of My Emotions

I give my experiences their value.

I can change my mood.

I can remain calm even when something bad happens.

Brain Rain: Emotional Thunderstorms

AN EMOTION CAN BE DEFINED as the process by which the brain determines or computes the value of a stimulus. Other aspects of emotions then follow this computation.

Western culture tends to describe destructive emotion as one that results in harm to oneself, others or property. Eastern culture describes it as one that disrupts the equilibrium of the mind or one's inner peace.

Here's how emotion works in our brains and bodies. Say you hit your thumb with a hammer. Nerves in your thumb, hand and arm send a pain signal to your brain. You almost immediately experience pain and yank your thumb away (your body's instinctive response to removing a hurt extremity from the source of danger). The progress of events—thumb tissue is injured, nerves fire, brain receives signal, muscles contract to quickly move the thumb—are steps of biochemical changes in the body's internal

> **In this session:**
> - Hit your finger/Hurt your feelings
> - Refractory period
> - Cycle of emotion
> - The meaning of events
> - Chemical construction of moods

43

physiology, your body's preconscious response to something it perceives as a crisis.

In these initial nanoseconds, emotions haven't kicked in yet. The overt bodily responses and associated pain are the advance guard of emotional responsiveness. It's only afterward (remember, we're talking nanoseconds) that a feeling emerges. This is the time during which you become aware that your brain has determined that something important is happening. Only then are your emotions aroused. In the case of hitting your thumb with a hammer, you're likely (although certainly not required) to start feeling anger and emotional pain.

Like the initial preconscious chain reaction, aroused emotions also trigger biochemical reactions in the brain that generate action—for example, jumping up and down and screaming some four-letter words. In reaction to both the preconscious response and the emotional response, we do things to cope with (or capitalize on) the external event that triggers us.

Next, there's a period of time that passes between the onset of the intense emotional reaction and the return to a state of relative emotional balance. This refractory period can last seconds, minutes or years. Positive Attitude Development helps reduce the intensity and length of the refractory period.

As hard as it may be to imagine, we can develop an attitude that delivers a different, unexpected emotional response. For example, after much training of his attitude, a Zen master might respond with laughter ("How silly of me to hit my thumb with a hammer!"), expressions of gratitude ("Thank goodness I didn't break the bone!") or no emotion at all ("This event has no meaning to me").

The cycle of our emotional reactions to situations, people, or events is not pre-determined or carved in stone. (After all, Zen masters are humans, too.) Through our life experience, we learn ways to respond to various stimuli. Remember Session 1?

Our brain develops its own unique neurological network, influenced by our unique daily experiences that trigger or inhibit our propensities. In a sense, during our time in the uterus, our DNA creates a brain ready to be programmed. Our experiences help program our neural networks as we grow through life. Our brains in turn adjust and adapt to help us address and/or survive our life experiences.

Sometimes, emotional reactions we would label destructive (like denial or apathy) work as short-term survival strategies to get us through immediate crises, especially when we're children. However, our past lessons about emotions are often inadequate for our present situations. What worked as a survival skill in childhood doesn't always work in adult society. The old attitude and emotional response habits must now be arrested and replaced with new constructive responses.

How do we do this? Once again, it comes down to developing a positive attitude by retraining our thoughts and beliefs to default into healthier patterns—at which point our behavior (and its consequences) also become healthier.

If the hammer doesn't hit your thumb very hard, then your pain (and the resulting anger) is likely to pass quickly—perhaps in a matter of seconds. You could be laughing about it five minutes later. This is because emotions come and go. When it comes to emotions, the sage is right when he says, "This, too, shall pass." However, we have to remember that this, too, shall pass applies to constructive emotions just as much as it does to destructive emotions. The attitude behind an emotion determines how long and how intensely that emotion will stick around. If you don't feed the supporting thoughts, the emotion will pass, no matter what it is.

When hammer and thumb make contact, getting angry and cursing may serve us well in the very short term. A yell and a hop can release the adrenalin-fueled muscle tension that's part of the body's preconscious response to pain. However, continued anger and curses are no help. They keep us stuck in a moment of emotional thunderstorm, even though the actual rain, thunder and lightening are long gone. It's as if we pull out our umbrella in the storm, but even after it's passed and the sun is shining, we hold on to the umbrella—and we keep the rain falling beneath it. We cut off our access to fully experiencing the moments happening afterward, including their potential for stimulating positive emotions within us. Too many of us feed our anger more often than necessary and stay angry far longer than will serve our best interests and well-being.

Remember that our thinking stream passes at enormous speed—60,000 thoughts a day. If we stop and just observe the stream, we remain calm. But if we grab on to any one negative thought, we're off on a rollercoaster ride. We feed that thought with others like it, and we're emotionally hooked. If we don't interrupt the pattern and detach—cold turkey—from the negative thoughts, we can spend minutes, hours, or even days, inflating the problem and knocking our lives off course.

The rollercoaster is easy to see in prison. Luis says something to Jerry and you can actually see Jerry get hooked—his body tenses, his stance alters, his tone of voice changes. In a split second, Jerry is caught by rage—and within a few minutes, his behavior might land him in solitary confinement.

You can probably see similar patterns around you at work or home. These knee-jerk reactions may seem unavoidable, but we actually do have other choices. Positive attitude lies in unhooking—that is, not getting attached to the thoughts either speeding or crawling by. Emotional detachment (which is not the same as apathy or amputation) is where balance, serenity and peace lie.

What we say and do influences how we feel as much as how we feel influences what we say and do. Feelings and actions reinforce each other.

BrainWork: Recognizing an Emotional Pattern

Hitting that thumb with the hammer is emotionally meaningless until we interpret the event and give it meaning. The meaning one person gives that event may be very different from the meaning someone else gives it; compare the angry, cursing guy to the Zen master.

When someone says or does something that hurts our feelings, what is it that hurts? Our emotional reaction may reach—or exceed—our emotional reaction after the hammer bruises our thumb. But when our feelings are hurt, no skin, muscles or nerves are damaged. So what is it that hurts, and why?

Prisoners commit suicide at higher than normal rates, whether at their own hands or through suicide-by-cop. Most of us can understand someone wanting to kill himself while living in captivity, a situation that appears hopeless.

But what about people who live in everyday society, where their freedom isn't restricted? Clearly, some of us humans despair no matter where we live. For me, a perfect example is Mr. G., who taught at one of the federal prisons where I used to live. Mr. G. always bragged about the beautiful woman he'd married. Then, one day, his wife left him. He came to work and broke down in tears during class. The prisoners told him, "C'mon, get it together. You can get another job or move someplace else. You've got your freedom, man! When one of us loses our woman, we have reason to be frustrated because there's no one else on the market! You can find another one."

However, Mr. G had built his entire sense of self on having this pretty woman in his life. Rationally, he should have been grateful for his freedom and the options available to him—especially after spending every work day among men with severely restricted freedom and options. Nevertheless, his negative thoughts and faulty beliefs took over. He was living his life for another person; when she left him, he thought and believed that the meaning of his life had disappeared as well. He couldn't get his thoughts in control, even though he had opportunity and freedom. The next day, he killed himself.

The point is this: Our circumstances don't determine our attitude, emotions or behavior. If we don't realize that our thoughts and beliefs can go over the top, we lose vigilance and our behavior can get so far out of control that our life ends. We have to understand the attitude, thoughts and beliefs stimulating our emotional reactions. When we change them, then the emotional

Your own moods can be extremely deceptive. They can, and probably do, trick you into believing your life is far worse than it really is. When you're in a good mood, life looks great. In good moods, things don't feel so hard; problems seem less formidable and easier to solve. When you're in a good mood, relationships seem to flow and communication is easy. If you are criticized, you take it in stride.
On the contrary, when you're in a bad mood, life looks unbearably serious and difficult. You have very little perspective. You take things personally and often misinterpret those around you, as you impute malignant motives into their actions.

—Richard Carlson, *Don't Sweat the Small Stuff*

reactions (along with their intensity and duration) change, too.

BrainWork: Recognizing Your Emotional Pattern

Our emotions have a kind of cycle or logarithm. Happy, sad, indifferent—feelings happen during the day like seasons move through the year. The logarithm is slightly different in each person, but there tends to be a consistent pattern for how the pharmacy in our brains distributes the chemicals that affect our moods. It's our privilege to learn how to alter that cycle through the mental exercises of PAD, so that we can improve the functioning of the brain's pharmacy. Knowing that the brain has plasticity, we can rework the chemical construction of our moods.

Summary

This lesson is about understanding the cycle of emotions and why we experience various moods. The paradigm of PAD brings forth the idea that chemistry, hormones and neurological activities are the precursors to feelings and behavior—and that we can alter them.

Recognizing an Emotional Pattern

This is a typical example of someone repeating old emotional patterns that translate into auto-pilot thinking and action that lead inevitably to difficulty.

BrainWork

THOUGHTS

Jerry comes to Wednesday night poker in a foul mood

He's acting oddly. I bet he thinks I cheated.

I shouldn't have told the guys he lost.

The rest of the guys are teasing Jerry about his big loss.

Jerry gets really defensive about his gambling skills, or lack of them.

ACTIONS

I win at poker, taking all of Jerry's money.

Jerry skips the regular Saturday morning golf game with the boys how I told the boys how I skunked him on Wednesday.

Jerry's compromising a work project because he's avoiding me.

THOUGHTS

The boss is looking at me funny. I bet he thinks I can't stand up for myself because Jerry is probably bragging about not paying me.

He keeps saying everything's fine, but he's avoiding me at work and socially. He hasn't paid his debt, either.

I'm being made to look like a fool. I think people are laughing at me now.

ACTIONS

The heck with Jerry and all the guys. I can't win no matter what!

Recognizing Your Emotional Pattern

Use this chart to plot out a time when your repetition of old emotional patterns translated into auto-pilot thinking and action leading inevitably to difficulty.

BrainWo

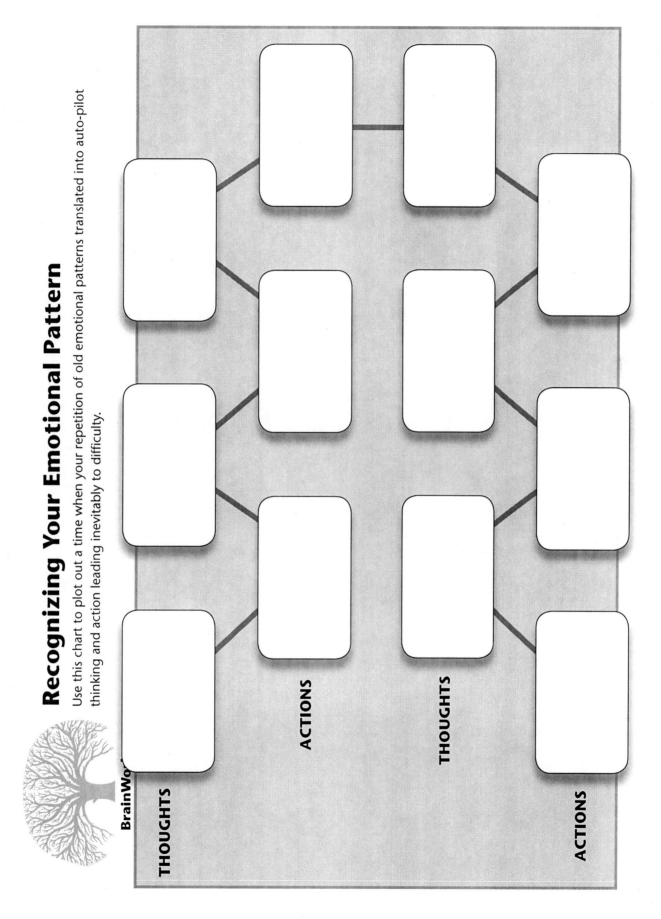

THOUGHTS

ACTIONS

THOUGHTS

ACTIONS

49

Direction

POSITIVE ATTITUDE DEVELOPMENT

Don't be a wandering generality;
be a meaningful specific.

—Zig Ziglar

◀ **ATTITUDE** ▶

I can let go, laugh, and move on.
I am determining my future.
I'm adding value.

> **In this session:**
> - A goal or a wish
> - Why and how of goals
> - What goals accomplish along the way

Setting Goals

IF YOU'RE OUTSIDE ON A SUNNY DAY, moving a magnifying glass all around, it doesn't serve much purpose. But hold very still and focus it on something flammable, and then what happens? That same magnifying glass can burn your house down.

Did you spend more time planning your wedding than you did planning your marriage? Have you spent more time planning vacations than planning your life? If so, you're not alone—even though such an approach to planning makes little sense. As we start to develop our attitude, beliefs and positive thoughts, we have to ask, what are we going to do with them? How will we make smart use of them? The next step is to put our attitude, beliefs and thoughts to work in achieving positive goals in our lives.

After a few weeks of taking the PAD course, a prisoner once told me, "It sounds like you're teaching us not to ask why something happened,

When I got my third DUI, I had no intention of stopping drinking. The judge told me I had two choices: 30 days in the workhouse or 90 days without alcohol and with 90 AA meetings. I'd done some time before, and didn't want to do any more—mostly because it interfered with my drinking. So I took option two, and started going to meetings. I had to get a meeting card filled out, so I could prove to the Probation Officer that I was going. I just sat and said nothing, fairly pissed off about having to be there. Nowhere on my radar was the goal of getting sober. I was only there for the judge.

But after a while, the things those AA people said starting sinking in. They told stories about themselves that made it damn near impossible to keep denying that I had a drinking problem. I still stayed dry because of the judge, but as the 90 days wore on, my girlfriend started saying how much more she loved me when I didn't drink. So after the 90 days was up, I kept going to meetings (and getting my card signed) for my girlfriend.

I went to meetings for about a year before I realized that I had started to be there—and be sober—for myself, not for the judge or my girl. It sounds weird to say, but that realization took me completely by surprise. Like I said, getting sober had never been my goal before—but suddenly it was now.

That was more than 15 years ago, and I still go to meetings. Even though I have no legal obligation anymore, I still bring a PO attendance

but instead to ask 'What now?'" There isn't much point in doing all this work to develop a positive attitude if we aren't going to build a better life with it. We now know how negative thoughts, beliefs and the resulting attitude have led us down a less-than-desirable life path. Look where we are now! The good news is that we can put positive thoughts, beliefs and resulting attitude to work today to plan a very desirable path for the rest of our lives.

Most inmates are in jail because of loose ends. Like Al Capone, the murderous crime boss who got nailed for failing to pay his taxes, they didn't follow through on tying up the straggling details and consequences of their actions.

But if we're honest with ourselves, most of us have to admit that criminals are not the only people who fail because they don't take care of life's loose ends. At least some of the time, all of us struggle to follow through in relationships and at work. We have trouble attaining our goals because we drop the ball on important details.

The idea of setting future goals may seem to contradict our emphasis on living in the current seven seconds. In practice, these aren't mutually exclusive activities. When we acquire the habit of living in the now, we start to understand that life's challenges, life's opportunities—even life itself—can't be permanently cured. The ideal life is not some immovable destination where we can arrive and say, "Ahhhhh. It's all better now; there's nothing more I need to do."

It's more useful to think of a meaningful life as a journey that unfolds before us. It's smart to have a map to guide our trip, but it's also smart to be prepared for detours, surprises and beautiful vistas that don't appear on the map. Setting a goal is like creating our own personal map. This may seem more challenging than stopping by the highway rest area for one of those free state maps—but it's also a lot more fun!

We start our map by imagining what goals we want to pursue. Imagining a goal starts with a dream: a desire for something we really want. Visualization of a goal (or anything else) is very powerful; it can direct our focus and channel our energies in ways we didn't think we were capable of.

But a goal isn't really a goal until the dream has a date. How do we get this date? It requires a plan—our road map to our destination. Motivation is the fuel that takes us there. Setting goals allows us to set our priorities and determine a direction we want to go.

BrainWork: Examining Your Successes

Goal setting is more than just a practical way to aim for something like a better career. It's also a key to happiness because it puts us into action. Action can remove the blues in ways that logic or talking alone can't. Setting and pursuing a goal provides some other concrete benefits:

- Keeps us on track

- Forces us to establish a direction

- Improves our self-esteem as we achieve small accomplishments along the way

- Makes us aware of our weaknesses

- Makes us aware of our strengths

- Brings to mind past victories, which energizes our present state of mind

- Defines reality and separates it from wishful thinking

- Sets a standard for our decision-making process (e.g., we must say no to certain things and yes to others).

card and get it signed. Those little cards remind me of three things: 1) life is so much better than it was 15 years ago, 2) if I do something good for someone else's benefit (like a judge or a woman), I may end up doing something good for my own benefit and 3) my goals change as I go along—and my achievements often end up being much greater than anything I had imagined when I started.

—John H.

This is a self-reinforcing process that supports positive attitudes and builds positive habits. An established habit is tough and resilient. We all know an alcoholic or drug addict who can tell us (and show us!) how a habit can be much stronger than reason, love or other powerful forces. However, habit is not the same as rigidity. When mapping and traveling toward a goal, we need to remain willing to be flexible and resilient—qualities that Positive Attitude Development enhances!

BrainWork: Your Successes and Your Future

Meaningful living demands that we establish goals and set off in a good, orderly direction to achieve them.

You must be before you can do, must do before you can have.

Summary

This lesson teaches how and why we should set goals to achieve meaningful living.

BrainWork

Examining Your Successes

Write down your thoughts about the questions below. Use another sheet of paper if you need it. After you've completed your answers, see page 90 to see some of our thoughts on the subject.

What is the difference between a goal and a wish?

_____

_____

Think of a time when you set a significant goal. Be specific and concrete in your answers. What was the goal?

_____

_____

What date did you set for attaining the goal?

_____

What obstacles did you have to overcome?

_____

What individuals, organizations and/or groups did you need to work with to accomplish the goal?

_____

What skills did you need?

_____

What was your plan?

_____

What was in it for you?

_____

_____

BrainWork

Your Successes and Your Future

Think of a significant goal you want to set for your future. Be specific and concrete in your answers. After you've completed your answers, see page 91 to see some of our thoughts on the subject.

What is the goal?

_____

_____

What date will you set for attaining the goal?

_____

What obstacles will you have to overcome?

_____

_____

What individuals, organizations and/or groups will you need to work with to accomplish the goal?

_____

What skills will you need?

_____

_____

What is your plan?

_____

_____

What's in it for you?

_____

_____

POSITIVE ATTITUDE DEVELOPMENT

Esteem

ATTITUDE

I have value.

I deserve good friends.

I respect myself.

I am not in this alone.

We have what we seek. It is there all the time, and if we give it time, it will make itself known to us.

—Thomas Merton

How You Matter

SELF-ESTEEM IS NOT MANUFACTURED BY FACTS, situations or experience, but rather on how we evaluate those facts, situations and experiences. In part, self-esteem is built on the feedback we get about our worth. We give ourselves some of that feedback. Other people give us feedback as well. We then interpret and evaluate what this feedback means about our concept of ourselves—our self-worth.

When we interpret the feedback from a negative perspective (with negative attitude, thoughts and beliefs), we give ourselves a poor sense of self. When we interpret the feedback from a positive perspective (with positive attitude, thoughts and beliefs), we give ourselves an enhanced sense of self.

When my prison sentence began, my self-esteem was based on what I had and who I knew. Of course, upon entering prison, I lost nearly all of my physical possessions. Very soon, the people I knew began falling away from my life as well. Because my self-esteem was so dependent on those external

In this session:

- Circles of self-esteem
- What we have
- What we leave behind
- The balancing act

things and people, it deflated like a balloon and I didn't know how to refill it. Each time another thing left my life, I descended deeper into a sense of worthlessness. As a result, I often struggled to get up in the morning and feel that I could accomplish anything that day.

BrainWork: Self-Esteem Spiral

After I went to prison, no one visited me—not even my brother or my fiancé. I kept hoping they would come and it hurt when they didn't. I joked that no one came because I had poor taste in friends. But deep inside, the empty visitors' room convinced me that I wasn't worth the trouble of visiting. It was nearly 12 years before I had my first visitor.

BrainWork: You and Your Self-Esteem

But during those 12 years, I learned an important truth: Self-worth is not built on the quality of what I do or don't possess or what does or doesn't happen to me. Remember, self-esteem is based on how I interpret those externals. The bottom line is that the quality of my personal possessions is beside the point. If I define myself by what I have or if I think the things I have are inferior, then I'll feel unworthy and be on my way to becoming an unlovable person.

Further reflection reveals that there are very few tangible things that can't be taken away from me. I can lose my car, my

wife, my kids, my freedom—even an eye or kidney. But I will still be me. And I will still have potential to become more than I am right now (more useful to others, more compassionate, more positive), even if I lose my limbs or spend the rest of my days incarcerated. The potential I have is never inferior.

What about people who don't go to the extremes listed in The Self-Esteem Spiral? A great many people have what we might call a run-of-the-mill sense of self. Their self-esteem is not too strong and not too weak, so they might seem to be in pretty good shape. But this is a case were the good is the enemy of the best. People like this are often like pinballs bouncing randomly around or sailboats without rudders. They fluctuate between feeling qualified and unqualified, appropriate and inappropriate. When presented with opportunity, they are uncertain and confused about their capability. While they may not feel that they deserve failure, they may also feel that they don't deserve to succeed, either.

It's a sad fact that many people go to their graves without ever making their unique contribution to the world. It's as if they misread the rhythms of their own possibilities and the measure of their own worth, so their music remains locked within, never added to the song of the universe.

BrainWork: Positive Self-Esteem

After six months in prison, I started volunteering for the prison's positive attitude class just to kill time. I didn't pay that much attention to the class or my instructor role; I just went through the motions and did what I was told. One day, another inmate told me, "Lyle, I'm trying to apply in my life some of the stuff you're teaching in that class. It really seems to be working!" I was shocked. I went back to my room and asked myself, "What does he mean? What did I do?"

Be not deceived; God is not mocked:
for whatsoever a man soweth,
that shall he also reap.

—Galatians 6:7

I didn't find an answer, but I kept on helping to teach the class, working a little harder to pitch the things the guy said were working for him. A few weeks later, another inmate came up and thanked me for what I'd been teaching, saying it's improving his life a lot.

I thought, "If it's working for these guys, maybe I should try it." So, it was really by accident that I started practicing these methods—even though (hypocritically) I was already preaching them.

I was happy with what I began to do, and even happier with the results I got. This was great, so I said, "I've got to do this again, to see if I'll feel the same way if I repeat the steps." I thought of it as a scientific experiment (after all, I was in prison after a career in underground chemistry!)

Repetition did work; the results were still wonderful. The experiments showed that I could trust this method and the universe. The pattern could be repeated with predictably reliable results. I could trust it

because it worked—just like I can trust nature to freeze water at 0° C.

When I started having new awareness, trusting in the universe, thinking and living in the moment, having honesty, integrity, understanding, compassion, and love—then I started to enjoy what I put out into the world, and my self-esteem started to build from within. My balloon started filling again.

But while our self-worth balloons may fill again, self-esteem is not the same as self-inflation. Strong self-esteem and meaningful living have their roots in humility. Humility requires understanding that we are one small part of the universe. In the big picture, one human's individual part is not the most important force in the universe—even the president of the United States is less powerful than the forces that hold a tiny atom together.

On the other hand, true humility is not the same as humiliation. While small, our place in the universe still has meaning. In other words, healthy self-esteem requires the humility of balance—living without either grandiosity or self-abasement. Humility, awareness, integrity, compassion and all the rest give us greater understanding of the deep hurts in life—like the fact that no one came to visit me in prison.

I eventually realized the problem wasn't that I had poor taste in friends. The problem was that I had compartmentalized my friends and never fully committed to them. I had one group of friends to drink with, another to drug with, a third to go to the movies with, and so on. I was too busy

> *Don't go around saying
> the world owes you a living.
> The world owes you nothing.
> It was here first.*
>
> **—Mark Twain**

being on the fly to do the steady, hard work of developing a deep bond with someone.

My life was not integrated and my relationships with friends weren't deep and meaningful—to me or to them. My commitment was so weak that, if I'd been on the outside and one of them had been in prison, I probably wouldn't have visited him either. This was a sad reflection on how I led my life, but I could cope with that kind of new awareness because my sense of self was growing stronger and I was growing more resilient and compassionate. I loved that feeling because no one could take it away from me—except me.

Healthy self-esteem allows us to live a life that is not at war with ourselves or other people. The more secure our self-worth, the more inclined we are to treat others with respect, compassion and good will, because we don't perceive them as a threat to us. We don't feel like strangers, afraid in a world we never made. We begin to respect ourselves—and self-respect is the foundation of respect for others.

Self-esteem grows through true, selfless service to people—including to ourselves. Such service is totally in our control, which means that our self-esteem is also in our control. You can keep building it every day, making it more and more healthy and resilient. In fact, self-esteem is like a muscle; if you don't exercise it every day, it atrophies.

Summary

This lesson teaches the power of self-esteem and the importance of understanding how it influences our choices. Understanding ourselves better makes it easier to understand and accept others.

If I continually reach out to others for love,
I am tipping forward, off center and unstable,
Leaning forward on whomever I contact,
And likely to fall flat and hard if the other leaves.

If I continually withdraw in fear,
I am tipping backward, tense and rigid,
And the slightest surprise will push me over.

If I feel uncertain in myself
And unstable in my base,
Then all my contacts with others
Will be wobbly and lack conviction.

In contrast, if I can become centered and balanced
In my own experience,
Then I can carry this moving center with me.

If I am balanced now,
Then I can move in any direction I wish
With no danger of falling,
And my contact with you is solid and real,
Coming to you from the root of my living.

—Barry Stevens and John Stevens
in *Embrace Tiger, Return to Mountain*
by Chunglaing Al Huang

BrainWork

Self-Esteem Spiral

How many of these outcomes in your own life have been influenced by negative self-esteem? Reflect on this for a few minutes before answering the questions on the next page.

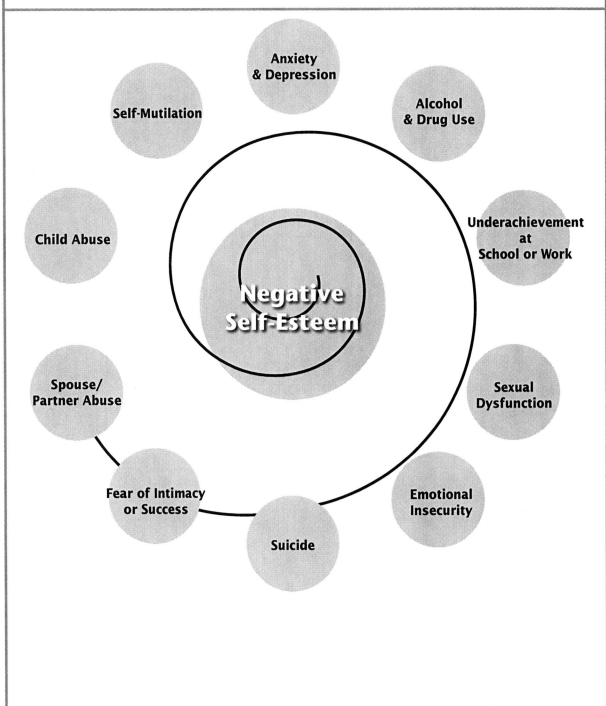

BrainWork

You and Your Self-Esteem

Write down your thoughts about the questions below. Use another sheet of paper if you need it. After you've completed your answers, see page 92 to see some of our thoughts on the subject.

How is your self-esteem affected by the following:

Who you gravitate to?

_____

Your use of time?

_____

The goals you reach for?

_____

How you treat others?

_____

The choices you make?

_____

What has been the connection between your potential and your self-esteem?

_____

How could a self-inventory affect your self-esteem?

_____

What do you think a good self-inventory should include?

_____

Do you think changing your self-esteem could make you uncomfortable?
Why or why not?

_____

BrainWork

Positive Self-Esteem

How many of these outcomes in your own life have been influenced, or might be influenced in the future, by positive self-esteem? Reflect on this for a few minutes in light of your answers from the last page.

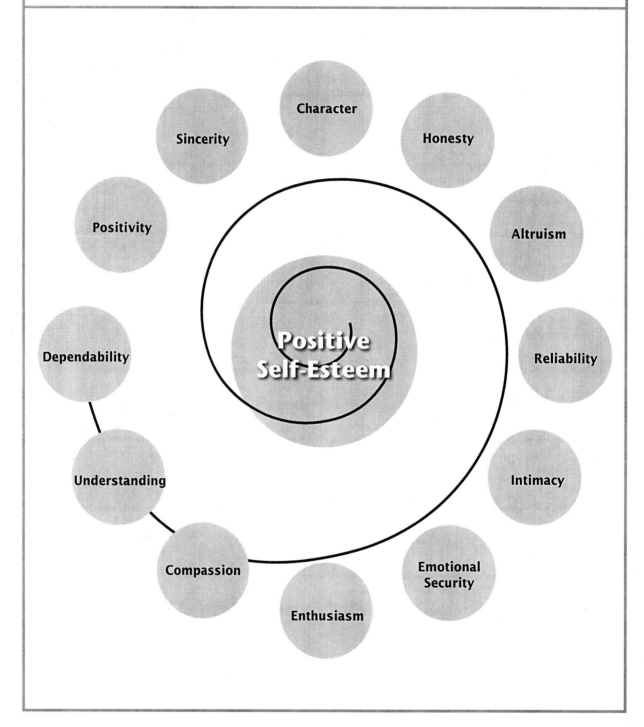

Sense

POSITIVE ATTITUDE DEVELOPMENT

◄ **ATTITUDE** ►

I can keep my head.

I can keep this going.

It makes sense for me to live better.

In this session:

- What's so funny?
- Making sense
- Core values
- Life tomorrow

Use Your Head

WHILE THIS IS THE LAST CHAPTER in this PAD workbook, your life is likely to continue tomorrow. Mine, too. So how can we keep developing positive attitude—and reaping its rewards—tomorrow and the day after that?

We've spent eight chapters working on our heads, reconstructing our attitude, thoughts and beliefs.

That process has developed our senses:

- Common sense
- Sense of awareness
- Sensible thinking
- Sense of trust
- Sense of time
- Sense of determination
- Sense of balance
- Sense of direction
- Sense of self

A common thread and common result of these characteristics is a sense of perspective.

This session discusses how to keep using our heads and nurturing the kind of sense that maintains positive attitude, thoughts and beliefs. After years of teaching PAD, it's become apparent to me and to previous students that a handful of characteristics are crucial to a meaningful, useful, and satisfying life. All of them feed a healthy attitude and perspective.

BrainWork: Core Value Inventory 1

So what are these essential characteristics that will help us transition from this PAD program into building a positive attitude for the rest of our lives? We call them our Eight Core Values.

1. Humor

2. Flexibility

3. Gratitude

4. Integrity

5. Patience

6. Understanding

7. Forgiveness

8. Love

Humor

Anger directed outward is violence.
Anger directed inward is depression
Anger deflected or defused is humor.

A sense of humor is evidence of perspective and healthy detachment. Humor, perspective and detachment are powerful ways to use your brain. They're like changing a diaper. It doesn't stop the poop from returning, but it makes everything look, smell and feel fresh for awhile.

[Humanity] has unquestionably one really effective weapon—laughter. Power, money, persuasion, supplication, persecution—these can lift at a colossal humbug—push it a little—weaken it a little, century by century; but only laughter can blow it to rags and atoms at a blast. Against the assault of laughter nothing can stand.

—Mark Twain, *The Mysterious Stranger*

Humor is not just powerful, it also helps give us perspective. A sense of perspective frequently returns the favor, by helping us have a sense of humor. With a sense of humor, we can look back at our past behaviors and chaotic experiences, see the impact they've had on our life and realize that we've survived them (and, in some cases, are better off).

Humor demonstrates and reinforces our willingness to let go of the negative beliefs, thoughts and perspectives that have damaged us in the past. Humor will help us in the future when we look back on the unexpected experiences we'll encounter as we approach the desirable future we're working to build with positive attitude, thoughts and beliefs. Indeed, even the universe has a sense of humor! We're better off when we can laugh along and keep our perspective, understanding that the universe was not designed for us individually but that we were designed for a useful role in the universe.

BrainWork: Rule # 62

A sense of humor and perspective show our capacity to roll with the punches and to be resilient and flexible. These are important traits to develop, since life isn't going to stop happening just because we're developing a positive attitude.

Flexibility

Scientists say that the only constant in the universe is change. Psychologists tell us that the one thing we can always expect from life is change. Change can come suddenly or it can crawl slowly along—revealed only after we have perceived small signs of it for days, months or even years. Fortunately, both we and the universe can be flexible enough to deal with any changes that come along.

Gratitude

When life becomes a journey and no longer a battle, we can begin to appreciate each moment and to be more grateful for it. In fact, each moment takes on a preciousness that lures us into participating more fully, with deeper trust. We are no longer bored or use statements like "killing time," "wasting time" or "passing time." We develop a gratitude that changes the texture of our lives.

Everyday life is an adventure filled with opportunities for us to become everything we can be. We can appreciate the gifts that come our way in the form of teachers or opportunities to teach. PAD's mental exercises help create ways to better appreciate the excitement in everydayness.

We are no longer fighting off life's experiences, but rather we are now faced with the opportunity to become artists designing our own lives.

Integrity

The glory which is built upon a lie soon becomes a most unpleasant encumbrance. How easy it is to make people believe a lie, and how hard it is to undo that work again!

—Mark Twain, *Mark Twain in Eruption*

The past eight sessions have helped us take an honest look at our attitude, thoughts, beliefs—an honest look at ourselves. Having perspective means taking an honest, open-minded look at the people and experiences around us. It also means acting with integrity and openness toward our fellows. Integrity is the structure through which we present ourselves. We realize the fallacies of deception and lies. We become drawn to the power of integrity and defend it through our interactions with others. Integrity becomes our love and as we court her throughout our lives, we become proud of the positive results integrity produces.

Patience

I have a friend who jokes, "I've thought about learning patience, but I don't have time for it." He also says that alcoholics, addicts and other self-absorbed people are "folks who think instant gratification takes too long."

Many of us have been driven by furious impatience in the past. But we've demonstrated our capacity for patience in PAD; it isn't easy to make radical changes in our attitude, thinking and beliefs, but we're doing it anyway. We can practice patience and understand that it is necessary for Positive Attitude Development and a quality life.

The fruits of patience are everywhere. Look at ancient cypress trees, the Rocky Mountains, the Grand Canyon, a rose, or even your children. They too develop through a long process and with patience. Likewise, we need patience as our attitude develops and becomes a valuable filter through which we view the world.

Understanding

When I was a teenager, I worried constantly about what people thought of me. When I reached my forties, I decided I didn't give a damn what people thought of me. At 60, I finally realized that most people had never been thinking about me at all. Like me, they were busy thinking about themselves.

—Anonymous

We're small on the scale of the universe, but we're not without meaning. The same thing holds true for everyone else in the universe. A strong sense of perspective and positive attitude depend on understanding our commonality with other people—even when those people are radically different from us (and/or drive us crazy!)

Understanding frees us to poke fun at

ourselves when we start thinking that our importance is so great that other people don't matter. It also helps us see how we are guests on this planet, with responsibilities to it, the people around us, the people who came before us and the people who come after us. Instead of becoming takers and killing the host upon which we live, understanding reveals that we and our host are all interconnected.

Forgiveness

None of us is qualified to define the world for anyone else. Even as we strive for peace of mind, gratitude and respect for others, we must learn other lessons as well:

- Live with a little ambiguity, instead of passing judgment on others.
- Take responsibility for our mistakes.
- Forgive the mistakes of others.

We have a perspective on the world. Some other people will share part or most of our perspective, while others will share none. But as the old saying goes, "Even a stopped clock is right twice a day."

We now realize that our reactions to other people and circumstances are the results of our own perspective, interpretation, thinking, beliefs—our own attitude. Other people don't cause our reactions, and they are not responsible for them. This realization is quite liberating—especially when we seize the opportunity to let go of past resentments, make amends for our own mistakes and forgive the mistakes of others.

Love

Love—a word that's often overused, abused or misunderstood. We use the same word

to describe how we feel about widely diverse things, from "I love applesauce!" to "I love my husband!" Still, love remains a powerful force in the world. The greatest of all emotions, love is the power that keeps reproducing itself, over and over.

Some neurologists believe that love can be profiled in the brain's landscape. If this is true, and love can be a neurological construction, then what stops us from developing the landscape?

Like any landscaping job, we have to diligently pull up weeds, and we have to guard against apathy, which saps the light and nutrients helping love grow. Of course, we may never be able to completely dissect love—and that's a good thing! Love remains an action, an emotion, an art, a connection, an instinct, a thought, a belief and an attitude.

When the moon reflects in the quietness of the lake, we can see it, but we're not able to reach down and capture it. Likewise the rainbow—we can see it and appreciate it; we can't touch it, but we can be touched by it. So it is with the mystery of life before our eyes. We can see it, but we can no more capture and hold it than we can capture and hold a ray of sun. We may hunger for it, but it's just a perspective away. This perspective can be developed through the mental exercises we've shared in these pages.

When we live positive core values, love becomes the filter through which we view our present seven seconds. It creates the texture of our self-talk, our conversation with others and our daily experiences. Love is a way of seeing that brings into view the mystery of life for each of us. Positive

Attitude Development allows us to encounter this mystery, which transforms our lives and reinforces the cycle of flexibility, humor, gratitude, integrity, patience, understanding, forgiveness and love. In the end, the more skilled we become in developing positive attitude, the greater is our capacity to love and our openness to another's love.

Even though this book is ending, you still have homework. The following pages hold some additional worksheets for you to use in the coming days and weeks; they focus on the core values we're discussing in this chapter.

In addition, I hope you'll review and re-use the BrainWorks from pervious sessions—along with this workbook—as you practice PAD and make your life better, more satisfying and more productive.

BrainWork: Core Value Inventory 2

Here are a couple of parting thoughts:

Like love,

. . . happiness isn't the result of good fortune or random chance. It isn't something that money can buy or power can command, nor is it dependent on external events. Instead, it depends on how we interpret external events. It's a condition we must prepare for, cultivate and personally defend. Those who control their inner experience will be able to determine the quality of their lives and that is as close as anyone can come to being happy.

—Mihaly Csikszentmihalyi,
Flow: The Psychology of Optimal Experience

BrainWork

Core Value Inventory 1

Write down your thoughts about the questions below. Use another sheet if necessary. When you have completed your answers, look at page 94 and see some of our thoughts on the subject.

What were your core values when you first started reading this book?

_____

_____

_____

What are your new core values? How are they different?

_____

_____

_____

If you were to die within the next week, what do you think your children, grandchildren or others would remember you for? How much do you think they would remember you at all?

_____

_____

_____

What do you *want* to be remembered for after you die?

_____

_____

_____

Rule # 62

BrainWork

Here's a story a co-founder of Alcoholics Anonymous tells about the early, exuberant days of AA in the 1940s when lots of eager groups were forming up:

A town we'll call Middleton figured it needed a great big alcoholic center, a kind of pilot plant AA groups could duplicate everywhere. Beginning on the ground floor there would be a club; in the second story they would sober up drunks and hand them money for their back debts; the third deck would house an educational project. In imagination the gleaming center was to go up several stories more, but three would do for a start. This would all take a lot of money . . . other people's money. Believe it or not, wealthy townsfolk bought the idea.

Of course there was a promoter in the deal . . . a super-promoter. By his eloquence he allayed all fears, despite advice from more experienced AA groups that ventures which mixed AA groups with medication and education had come to sticky ends elsewhere. To make things safer, the promoter organized three corporations and became president of them all. Freshly painted, the new center shone. The warmth of it all spread through the town. Soon things began to hum. To

insure foolproof, continuous operation, 61 rules and regulations were adopted.

Well, things didn't work out quite how the organizers, funders—and the super-promoter—had planned. Some drunks came for the education programs, but refused to admit they had a drinking problem. Some insisted that a cash loan would solve all of their problems—but it seldom did. Others joined the club, when they were really just looking for a quick romance. Some ended up hospitalized or in trouble with authorities—damaging the center's reputation in town.

Sure, there was a ton of activity going on, but it proved the old adage: "Motion doesn't necessarily bring Progress." The inevitable explosion ensued, leaving everyone feeling frustrated and afraid. Finally, the head promoter admitted that he should have listened to more experienced AAs, who advised him to "keep it simple" and did something else that was to become an AA classic. It all went on a little card about golf-score size. The cover read: "Middleton Group No. One. Rule No. 62." Once the card was unfolded, a single pungent sentence leaped to the eye: "Don't take yourself too damn seriously."

—adapted from AA's
Twelve Steps, Twelve Traditions

Rule # 62 *continued*

When you have completed your answers, look at page 94 and see some of our thoughts on the subject.

Give an example of how someone you know took themselves too seriously.

_____

_____

_____

_____

_____

_____

_____

_____

_____

List some benefits that come from having a sense of humor.

_____

_____

_____

_____

_____

_____

_____

_____

_____

BrainWork

Core Value Inventory 2

Write down your thoughts about the questions below. Use another sheet if necessary. When you have completed your answers, look at pages 95–98 and see some of our thoughts on the subject.

Flexibility

What issues have you been too rigid on?

_____

How can you be less rigid?

_____

Stop for a moment and practice mental flexibility. What does it look like?

_____

Gratitude

What is the difference between appreciation and expectation?

_____

_____

What do you have appreciation for today that you once despised?

_____

What are three things you appreciate today?

_____

What can you be grateful for that you overlooked in the past?

_____

_____

Core Value Inventory 2 *continued*

Why didn't you notice these precious moments before?

_____

What are three things you are grateful for today?

_____

Integrity

What does it mean to have integrity?

_____

What are some ways you can live with integrity?

_____

What are some ways you've showed integrity in the last 24 hours?

_____

Patience

What have you lost because you didn't have patience?

_____

How can you be more patient?

_____

What are some ways you can visualize yourself being patient when you usually aren't?

_____

_____

Core Value Inventory 2 *continued*

Understanding

Why is understanding important?

_____

How can you be more understanding?

_____

What is something you could be more understanding about in your life today?

_____

Forgiveness

In what areas of life are you most judgmental?

_____

Why do you feel you have the right interpretation?

_____

What is an issue in your life you could view with a different perspective?

_____

Love

Discuss love as an emotion.

_____

How is love influenced by the person giving the love?
By the person who is receiving the love?

_____

_____

What difference, if any, do you see between the function of love and the art of love?

_____

Afterword

WE HOPE THAT YOUR LIFE HAS BEEN TOUCHED by our Positive Attitude Development program. We know PAD is not the only way to encounter the mystery of life, but it is one that has worked for thousands of prisoners—including lifers—many of them living in deep pain and despair, and a growing number of participants in the outside world.

It has transformed lives (including my own) and eliminated an emptiness that felt like it could never be filled. With this sense of fulfillment and the tools to recreate it daily, people like you and me have found bliss and beauty where we'd never seen it before—in the everydayness of life. May you enjoy this journey of discovery forever.

Thank you for participating in the PAD program.

—Lyle

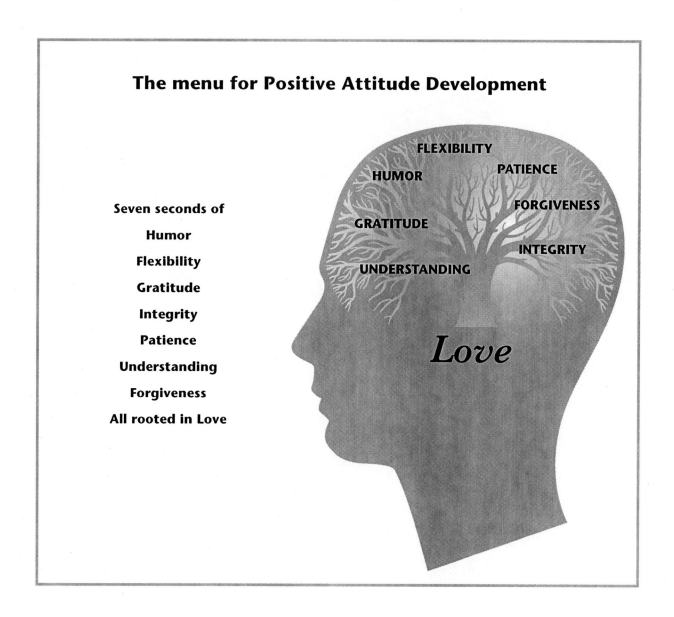

The menu for Positive Attitude Development

Seven seconds of

Humor

Flexibility

Gratitude

Integrity

Patience

Understanding

Forgiveness

All rooted in Love

FLEXIBILITY

HUMOR

PATIENCE

FORGIVENESS

GRATITUDE

INTEGRITY

UNDERSTANDING

Love

Worksheet Answers and Comments

p. 13

BrainWork: Beliefs

How do you believe a person's attitude relates (if at all) to a person's fate?
Our attitude is directly related to the outcome of our lives. Our attitude is the cloud from which our thoughts rain. Those thoughts nourish the soil from which our actions grow and our actions then produce our destiny. We tend to think of our fate as something that is out of our control and happens TO us. But we have a lot more control over our future than we usually think we do—which is why it helps to think of the future in terms of destiny (which we can influence) rather than fate (something in which we're passive participants).

How do you believe that what people say to themselves—the thoughts they express—relate to their fate?
Thoughts run in patterns, most of them unconscious. Even negative, self-destructive thoughts stick around in our brains because the old problematic brain pathways are well-worn and comforting in their familiarity. To change our fate or destiny, we have to change our behavior. To change our behavior, we have to change the workings of our brains—to change the processing system originally developed in response to our life experiences. That's why PAD is so important.

What are some of your beliefs and thoughts about your current life situation?
Given your past and present, you might think and believe things like this:

> Life is a constant battle and I always have to watch my back.
> The surest (or only) way to get ahead is to take from someone else or put them down.
> I'll never get enough of what I need.

By the time you're done with this book, you may start to have different thoughts and beliefs, such as:

> Life is a journey and not a battle
> No one has to lose for me to win.
> Life has abundance for everyone

List three positive ways you could use the power of your thoughts.
Here are just a few examples:

> To create hope
> To change habitual ways of thinking

To create confidence and a good sense of self worth
To grow close to other people
To have fun and freedom in my life

Nine dot puzzle answer explanation

Most people find this puzzle impossible to solve. The reason is pretty simple—and illustrates how quickly and deeply a pattern of thinking gets lodged in our brains.

When we look at this puzzle, most of us (unconsciously) impose a square box on the picture—a box made from four invisible lines along the "edge" of the puzzle. Thinking this way about the situation, we develop the belief that we can't draw any lines outside of that invisible square. But, as you can see below, the solution requires that we extend some of the lines beyond the invisible box we imposed. To quote the old cliché, we have to "think outside the box."

We can work on the puzzle for hours, demonstrating tons of good will, determination and persistence. Those qualities are positive and admirable, but, on their own, they are inadequate to the situation. That's because our "we have to stay inside the (invisible) box" thinking and beliefs make it impossible to connect all nine dots with only four straight lines. We can't solve the puzzle using our existing pattern of thinking.

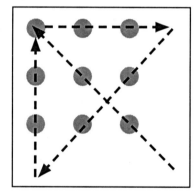

This puzzle is a simple illustration of why it's so important for us to develop new attitudes, thoughts and beliefs—so that we have more capacity to successfully deal with the new and surprising situations life has in store for us.

p. 15

BrainWork: Choices

Describe a time when your past negative attitudes and thought processes influenced your choices.

Here are some common examples I heard during my 18 years of teaching PAD in federal prisons:

When I got disgusted with having a job and chose to become an underground chemist manufacturing synthetic cocaine.

When I got fed up with my girlfriend/wife because I thought she was impossible, I chose to sleep around—and lost my girlfriend/wife.

Prison is a waste of time. Nothing good can happen here. My life is on hold until I get out.

What beliefs hijacked your thoughts in that situation?

Again, here are some common answers I've heard from other PAD participants.

I was too important to be just a worker. That the profits would make my life better. That I would never get caught. That dealing drugs would stick it to "the man."

That things would never improve in our relationship. I deserved to get my sexual urges met, no matter what. My worth as a man depended on how often I scored.

Things will never get any better. I'm not part of the in crowd and people will never let me forget where I came from. I'm trapped in the same place.

List some different beliefs that might have brought about better results for you.

Being dishonest in business destroys my reputation and hurts people. I can use my energy and money more productively if I'm honest.

Relationships have ups and downs. Sex is only one dimension of real intimacy and fulfillment. The love I've earned from my significant other is an expression of my value to him/her.

There are opportunities everywhere. I can find and use them. I can read, take courses, practice PAD, work on my relationships and learn what I need to know to advance in my chosen field of endeavor.

p. 16

BrainWork: Choices *continued*

Fill in these circles with some beliefs that hijack your thoughts today.
Here are some common examples I heard from other PAD participants.

Nobody loves me
They're out to get me
I'm a piece of shit
I'm better than they are
I deserve what I want, when I want it
Nobody understands me
In the end, people will always let me down
You can't really trust anyone
I don't deserve to be here
I'm always getting screwed
I'm surrounded by idiots
I can stop drinking/using anytime I want

p. 17

BrainWork: Choices *continued*

Is your destiny the result of your past thoughts?
Up to now, yes. Our thoughts nourish the soil from which our destiny emerges. Thinking determines behavior, which determines destiny. To change behavior we have to change the workings of our brains—to change the processing system we're using now or have used in the past. With practice, we can train our brains to prune unused dendrites (the parts of nerve cells that produce impulses) and delete those parts that reinforced our old negative behavior. We can reinforce new neural activity to support the behavior we want and need—and that will produce a positive destiny for us.

Why do some people see the glass half-full and others see it as half empty?
Some see the glass half-full because they are filling the glass. They live in a world of abundance. They tend to be givers. Those who see the glass half-empty are drinking from it and live a world of scarcity. They tend to be takers and hoarders. Our attitude, thoughts and beliefs set the patterns that make us either optimists or pessimists.

What is an attitude?
Pioneering psychoanalyst Carl Jung defined attitude as: A readiness of the psyche to act or react in a certain way. Webster's Dictionary describes it as a mental position with regard to a fact or state; a feeling or emotion toward a fact or state; or a state of readiness to respond in a characteristic way to a stimulus (such as an object, concept, or situation).

Since an attitude doesn't have external, physical substance that we can examine and touch, it's hard to describe in words. Paradoxically, we still know an attitude when we see and feel it. PAD believes that attitudes develop from our core values—and that our attitudes produce a stream of matching thoughts and beliefs that nourish our actions—and, thus, our destiny.

p. 24

BrainWork: What Are You Thinking?

What's the first thought that comes to mind when you see each of these words?
Here are some common examples I heard from other PAD participants.

Anger: Someone's always pushing my buttons. People make me mad. It's someone else's fault.

Sex: Relief. Release. Instant gratification. Never enough of it.

Betrayal: Unfair. The story of my life. Abandonment. Why I'm in this mess in the first place.

Joy: It's not really possible. Joy is fake and never real. Getting high.

Love: Impossible. It's really an illusion. You can't trust anyone.

Forgiveness: I deserve it but others don't. You can't forgive and forget. Some things you just can't ever forgive.

Here are some alternative ways to think about these words:

Anger: The cork that keeps every other emotion stuffed inside. Anger is my choice—no one can make me mad. Anger is an understandable first response—but dangerously corrosive to hang onto over time.

Sex: One aspect of intimacy, among many others (like psychological, emotional and spiritual connection). Not the only way to express love and tenderness. Sex can't sustain a relationship on its own. It demonstrates the possibility that one can totally accept another person.

Betrayal: Violation of trust. Betrayal will happen to me (since people are imperfect) but that doesn't mean I'm abandoned by everyone. What looks and feels like betrayal may be something less serious (like simple thoughtlessness). Betrayal can be information to help me know who I can really trust.

Joy: I can feel joy here and now. It does exist. I can be happy and have good times, no matter what the circumstances.

Love: I am lovable, and people (including me) are capable of loving unconditionally. Love is always nonviolent.

Forgiveness: A process, not an event. Forgiving is difficult (but not impossible) and, ultimately, always necessary to achieve freedom and happiness.

What do you think it means to begin a new life?
PAD demonstrates that we can re-create our lives and change our destiny if and when we begin to adjust our attitudes, thoughts, beliefs and actions.

How can you begin a new life in your current situation?
By choosing to develop new habits and arrest any negative thinking. The decision to do this is NOT dependent on my surroundings or circumstances.

Do you need to forget the past to begin a new life?
No. But we do need to discard the belief that our past completely determines our present and future. The past can inform our present and provide clues for what to do—and not do—in order to improve our present and future.

How important is forgiveness in beginning a new life?

Forgiveness is essential for creating a new life. Without it, we remain stuck in the past and its old thinking patterns. But forgiving usually requires changing our thoughts, attitude, values and beliefs. In fact, applying PAD methods to our memories of past events can actually change how we interpret their meaning today.

Are there any actions that you just can't forgive? If so, what are they?

We believe it is possible to forgive anything—and that the act of forgiving past violations is in our hands, not anyone else's. To forgive requires only one person. Forgiving doesn't mean we condone someone else's wrong actions—but it does mean we stop choosing to have those actions control any part of our lives today. True forgiveness brings liberation because, as a sage once said, "Resentment is the sword with which we pierce our own souls." However, it is very difficult to forgive past actions if we maintain the same old core values and beliefs. On the other hand, forgiveness of someone else is ultimately a gift we give to ourselves.

What purpose does it serve to bury the hatchet if you're going to mark the spot?

None (I bet that answer didn't surprise you!). If you keep returning to a past violation in your mind or conversations, that's evidence that you haven't finished the forgiveness process—and you haven't freed yourself from your pattern of resenting and feeling "controlled" by past events. Marking the spot where you buried the hatchet is the first step on a path to going back and repeating old behaviors. If nothing changes, nothing changes.

If we don't learn from the past are we condemned to repeat it?

Yes. If we don't learn from our mistakes we will keep repeating them and keep getting the same old outcomes. Just remember that popular definition of insanity: doing the same thing over and over, yet expecting different results.

p. 29

BrainWork: Susceptibility Scan

Write out the words associated with the letters below.

S. Susceptible	S. Susceptible
N. Negative	P. Positive
I. Influences	I. Influences
O. Other	O. Other
P. People	P. People

Who did Morris Goodman repel SNIOP in his recovery?

He didn't let his thoughts, beliefs and actions be determined by what the professionals around him thought, believed or did. He chose not to accept or internalize a paradigm that said he couldn't recover.

Morris put himself on a strict mental diet—but it wasn't a diet of deprivation. What kind of nourishment did Morris feed his brain while on his mental diet?

He feed his brain positive, hopeful, expectant, and constructive thoughts. He also reached out to bring positive, hopeful, expectant, and constructive people (like his sister) close by to support him.

Give some examples of negative influence you have to overcome in your life.

Here are some common examples from other PAD participants.

> People saying that I would never amount to anything.
> People saying I couldn't be successful with my past.
> The negative influences of my environment.
> The belief I would never find a good job or relationship.

What negative influences if any, will you experience in the future?

Here are some common answers I heard while teaching PAD.

> People who complain but never change.
> People who give up to stay where they are, instead of giving up to move on.
> My own thinking patterns when I'm not vigilant about keeping my thoughts, attitudes and beliefs positive.

p. 30

BrainWork : Beliefs, Thoughts and Actions

What do you think would have happened to you if you had been in an accident like Morris Goodman had?

Here's the most common answer I heard while teaching. "I would have given up and died." But I'm not convinced that's what most of us would actually do. For example, I was in a serious auto accident several years before I went to prison. I was pronounced dead shortly after arrival. Even without fully understanding what I was doing, I believed in the power of my thinking. I knew there was a way out of that mess and that I wouldn't give up. I didn't give up and eventually I recovered. On the down side, the surgery and recovery exposed me for the first time to mind-altering chemicals (triggering an unhealthy fascination with them)—but the point is that we often have more capacity for survival and recovery than we realize.

What would your beliefs, thought and attitudes have been in that situation?
Here is an answer I heard while teaching PAD.

The odds are too great and the doctors are right. I would give up and die.

What is the difference between those beliefs, thoughts and attitudes and the ones that Morris seems to have in his recovery?
Instead of giving up or giving in to negative thoughts, beliefs and attitudes, Morris chose another path. He believed in the power of his thoughts. He believed that he can overcome situations like a serious illness and that circumstance alone will not dictate his future.

Put these differences into these three categories.
For example, you might write:

Beliefs	Attitudes	Thoughts
Me: This accident will destroy me	This is way too hard	There's no way I'll recover
Morris: I will survive this accident	I can change my thoughts	I will recover

p. 33

BrainWork: Zeroing in on Now

Here's one example of the thoughts a PAD participant had during a 10-second period:

This is silly.

I'm hungry.

Where is my girlfriend?

My foot itches.

Will I get a letter today?

Is time up yet?

I want coffee.

p. 34

BrainWork: Fear Factors

How do you define fear?

F. alse	F. antasy
E. vidence	E. xperiences
A. ppearing	A. ppearing
R. eal	R. eal

Describe a time when false or fantasized experiences appeared real in your life.
Here are some examples from past PAD participants:

When I thought someone's facial expression or tone of voice meant they were mad at me.

When I was convinced that my wife was cheating on me, even though she really wasn't.

When I thought a guard was coming after me, when it turned out that he was just walking by.

If you knew you were going to die tonight what would you do with the rest of today?
Some examples from past PAD participants:

I'd get as high as I could or have as much sex as I could.

I would keep living my normal life because I believe it contains the quality of life I enjoy and want.

Now think about the legacy you want to leave your loved ones. If you knew you were going to die tonight, what would you do with the rest of today?

Some examples from past PAD participants:

Walk my talk because I want my kids to do that and believe that I did it.

Write or call my kids to tell them how much I really love them.

Thank people for how they've helped me.

p. 38

BrainWork : A Vocabulary Diet

How are you tested or challenged every day?
All of us are challenged by changes that happen to one degree or another every day. We can

be challenged by another person's behavior, like believing that a friend has betrayed us or that my business partner wants to cut me loose. We are tested every day in our journey to reshape or attitude, thinking, beliefs and behaviors.

Certain words or phrases promote failure. What words or phrases have you heard other people use that you think have promoted failure in their lives?
Some examples from past PAD participants:

> I can't, I quit, yes, but…, no use trying, unable, can not, impossible, out of the question, failure, hopeless situation, improbable, not me, not my problem, never been done before.

What words or phrases have you used that you think have promoted failure in your life?
Some examples from past PAD participants:

(See the answers to the last question!)

What things do you tell yourself that erode your motivation?
I don't know how to do this. It's never been done before. I'm too old. People don't care anyway. It's a waste of time. If it was possible, someone else would have done it already.

What words or phrases do you need to remove from your vocabulary to help you reach your goals?
The best place to start is by removing the phrases you listed in the last three questions. Use those lists to help police your thinking.

Which of these statements do you believe?
The correct answer is B. Failure is not genetic. It is a learned behavior—which means we can change it by shifting to positive attitudes, thoughts and beliefs.

p. 39

BrainWork: Determining Your Success

What have you given up on in the past that, upon reflection, you could have accomplished if you'd persisted?
Some common answers include:

> A relationship
>
> Reading a book
>
> Winning a competition
>
> Finishing high school
>
> Finishing college

What are some small steps you've taken to reach a goal?

This list might include things like:

Set a date to accomplish my goal

Listed the obstacles I have to overcome

Listed the groups, organizations, and individuals I can (or have to) work with

Listed the skills necessary

Made a daily, weekly, and monthly plan

Listed why I want this goal

What's a positive way to perceive obstacles and adversity?

Obstacles and adversity are inevitable, no matter what our situation. Rather than resenting them, it helps to see them as opportunities and challenges which can help motivate taking steps toward success.

Is life like the Super Bowl—does your winning depend on someone else losing?

No. Think about it like a parent. Making one of your kids fail is not the way to help another of your kids to succeed. The more people I help become successful the more successful I will become.

What other ways might there be to perceive success?

The feeling you have accomplished something worth while

Identifying success before you start your journey

A happy relationship with your partner and a well integrated family

Being of service to others, without expecting any reward

Doing the right thing when no one is watching

p. 41

BrainWork: Tracking Your Personal Development

What are examples of what you've learned in some of the peaks and valleys of your life?

Peaks: Just as in hard times, when it comes to good times, This too shall pass. That means enjoy and appreciate them as they happen. The memory and inspiration of life's peaks can sustain me in the valleys. There is always something for which to be grateful in life—including life itself.

Valleys: This too shall pass. Important life lessons for personal growth happen in the valleys. In the valleys, I have learned that persistence is important. Trust is the key for creativity and resilience. Life has never given me more that I can handle, but sometimes it has taken all I have. And that's OK.

p. 55

BrainWork: Examining Your Successes

What is the difference between a goal and a wish?
A goal has a date for it to be accomplished. A wish is just a statement.

Think of a time when you set a significant goal. Be specific and concrete in your answers. What was the goal?
Some goals that past PAD participants listed include:

>To read 50 pages of nonfiction everyday

>To complete (and do well in) a course

>To develop a relationship with a life partner who has similar core values.

>To write a book.

>To learn carpentry

What date did you set for attaining the goal?
The choices can run any realistic length of time:

>By the end of each day.

>By the end of the year

>In five years' time.

What obstacles did you have to overcome?
>My laziness and finding the books

>Family objections or apathy

>The urge to get into a relationship with the first person I met

What individuals, organizations and/or groups did you need to work with to accomplish the goal?
>Friends who could share their books with me

>The library staff

>Chaplains, AA/NA group leaders and other volunteers

>People who can supplement my skills or teach me the skills I need

>Educators

What skills did you need?
Past PAD participants listed things like:

I had to learn to read and concentrate in spite of noises

Learned how to improve the curriculum of my class

I had to learn to directly ask for—and accept—help from others

What was your plan?
Past PAD participants listed things like:

I determined to read three times during every day

Practice, Practice, practice

Become friends with someone before thinking about getting romantically involved with them

What was in it for you?
Past PAD participants listed things like:

Peace of mind and knowledge that no one could take it from me

A way to expand my horizons

Enjoy a wonderful relationship

p. 56
BrainWork: Your Successes and Your Future

Think of a significant goal you want to accomplish. Be specific and concrete in your answers.

Below is my own example of how I set and managed the goal of developing the PAD course in prison—and for after my release.

What is the goal?
I want to help others challenge their belief systems and thus change the way they see the world.

What date will you set for attaining the goal.
I have set a series of short term goals. I will have my book published before the end of 2008.
I will have a web site developed by Nov. 2008.
I will have an e-learning video completed by Jan. 2009.

What obstacles will you have to overcome?

I will have to generate enough funding to complete this task.

I will have to find the right people to help me.

I will have to practice so I am the best at what I do.

What individuals, organizations and/or groups will you need to work with to accomplish the goal?

A web-based learning service

Men as Peacemakers

A professional writer

Whole Person Associates

Corporations and NGOs

Local leaders

What skills will you need?

Public speaking skills

Speech writing skills

Communication skills

What is your plan?

To follow all of the steps laid out above

What's in it for you?

I will feel that my life is more meaningful because I will have changed the world for the better. I will continue to grow along my own journey of Positive Attitude Development by practicing and working on it every day. I will be of service to others.

p. 63

BrainWork: You and Your Self-Esteem

How is the following affected by your self-esteem?

Who you gravitate to?

Folks tend to gravitate to those who think like they do and those with whom they have things in common. So, if I think positively, I'll gravitate toward others who do—and if I gravitate toward people who already think positively, that will reinforce my positive thinking.

Your use of time?

We use our time to accomplish the tasks most important to us. If I waste my time—use it to accomplish little or nothing—that is strong evidence that I haven't really made accomplishment a priority. Spending time meeting positive goals—and spending time around peers who also work toward positive goals—has a direct impact on my sense of self-worth.

The goals you reach for?

I can't reach beyond the limitations I set inside of myself. For example, I cut off the option of working someplace with computers if I believe that I can never learn to type. I set out to accomplish those goals that match my self esteem.

How you treat others?

The way I treat others tends to reflect the way I see and treat myself. If I despise myself, I tend to despise others. If I see myself as inferior, I tend to think of everyone else as significantly better—or worse—than me. Practicing generosity and forgiveness with others can help me learn to be generous and forgiving with myself.

The choices you make?

The choices I make reflect my self-esteem and my perception of my internal limitations and potential. It doesn't even occur to me to pursue a goal if my thinking and belief tell me that such a goal is beyond my reach—even though the goal may (in reality) be well within my reach.

What has been the connection between your potential and your self-esteem?

What I see as my limitations tends to be fed by my self esteem, and vice versa. The same is true with what I see as my potential.

How could a self-inventory affect your self-esteem?

It is one way to do an honest, judgment-free assessment of my assets and liabilities. Reflecting on that balance sheet can help me rethink the self image I have created in the years of my growing up. It also helps me set goals for making amends, reducing my liabilities, and nurturing my assets.

What do you think a good self-inventory should include?

The most useful self-inventories include an evaluation of core values. Ask how you acquired your core values and why you still hold them. Ask:

What results are you getting in your life and what are you getting out of those results?

Do you want the results that are coming your way?

What results, if any, would you like to be different?

Do you think changing your self-esteem could make you uncomfortable? Why or why not?

Absolutely yes. Any major change in how we think, feel, act, and live will trigger some level of temporary discomfort. Think of the discomfort you felt when you moved your hands into a different position at the beginning of this workbook. But change's discomfort is not a sufficient excuse to forego the benefits of positive change.

p. 71

BrainWork: Core Value Inventory 1

What were your core values when you first started reading this book?

Past PAD participants have written things like this:

> Pleasure, money, power, instant gratification, looking out exclusively for my own individuals interests

What are your new core values? How are they different?

Past PAD participants have written things like this:

> Freedom, transparency, honesty, integrity, compassion, understanding and love

If you were to die within the next week . . .

Past PAD participants have written things like this:

> They would probably remember me for my old life more than my new one since I haven't had time to prove my new life.

> I hope they will remember how things have started to get better and that I'm more responsible and caring toward them. I want my actions to show them that I truly am doing the best I can now.

What do you want to be remembered for after you . . .

One PAD participant wrote:

> I would like to be remembered for setting a new course for my life (despite my mistakes in the past) and that my new life was an honorable one.

p. 73

BrainWork: Rule #62

Give an example of how someone you know took themselves too seriously.

Previous PAD participants have written:

ME! I used to (and still do sometimes) actively look for occasions to feel dissed. It's like I needed someone to disrespect me in order to prove to myself that I deserve respect. That's taking myself so seriously that it's crazy!

Some of my friends get instantly offended if I offer to help them. It seems like they think I'm questioning their ability. It's so much easier to be around people when they lighten up and see the absurdity in everyday life.

List some benefits that come from having a sense of humor.
Here are some expected—and unexpected—benefits:

Your digestive system works better.

Your risk of heart disease decreases.

Your overall health improves.

You have a better perspective on life (your own and other people's).

You see things more realistically.

p. 74

BrainWork: Core Value Inventory 2

Below are some common responses that past PAD participants gave to the questions on pages 74, 75 and 76:

Flexibility

What issues have you been too rigid on?
   What I expect of others

   My own perfectionism

   How I think other people should act and live

How can you be less rigid?
   By allowing others to act the way they want

   By not asking or expecting other people to make their decisions based on what I want

   By accepting people and situations for who and what they are

   By saying the Serenity Prayer a lot

Stop for a moment and practice mental flexibility. What does it look like?

It seems to change my world, my emotional balance and my sense of well-being.

I see people differently and with more tolerance.

I allow the world and everyone in it to be whoever they want.

I can discuss issues, but it's okay if not everyone sees everything my way.

Gratitude

What is the difference between appreciation and expectation?

Appreciation is enjoying what you have, but expectations are likely to put me in conflict with want is actually going to happen. Let go and let others live.

What do you have appreciation for today that you once despised?

My friend's interaction with me. I don't expect them to act a certain way and now I have gotten to know them much more and enjoy our relationship more, too.

What are three things you appreciate today?

My health

Friends

New opportunities I have discovered

The fact that I'm alive

My family

What can you be grateful for that you over looked in the past.

The kindness of others

The quality of intimate relationship

All the help I have received from others

The trust of others

Insights about life

p. 75

BrainWork: Core Value Inventory 2 *continued*

Why didn't you notice these precious moments before?

Because I was too focused on my expectations—how I thought life ought to be.

What are three things I am grateful for today?

My health

Friends

New opportunities I have discovered

The fact that I'm alive

My family

Integrity

What does it mean to have integrity?
Being trustworthy in choices and behaviors.

Being rigorously honest with myself and others.

What are some ways you can live life with integrity?
Say no to the things that are in conflict with your core values.

Act in accordance with your core values.

Be rigorously honest with myself and others.

What are some ways you've showed integrity in the past 24 hours?
I have been transparent when asked about my past.

I have spent time helping someone else and not focused on me.

I took a moment and reevaluated my core values.

Patience

What have you lost because you didn't have patience?
A past relationship

A job

Chances to make money

The ability to do more for my family

How can you be more patient?
By understanding there is a time for things to develop and there are times to push

By remembering that I'm not the center of the universe

By remembering that things take time

What are some ways you can visualize yourself being more patient when you usually aren't?

By listening openly when someone challenges me in a discussion

By taking deep breaths and appreciating what's going on when my kid is learning something new.

By taking deep breaths and appreciating what's going on when I'm learning something new.

p. 76

BrainWork: Core Value Inventory 2 *continued*

Understanding

Why is understanding important?

It allows us to have a more realistic perspective on events

It helps me get closer to other people, like my wife, and feel safer with them

How can you be more understanding?

By being more patient

By remembering the golden rule—treat others like I want to be treated

What is something you could be more understanding about in your life today?

About how hard it is for my wife and family to live everyday while I'm traveling and/or working so much

About the way things take time to develop and that you can't always push everything to happen on your schedule

Things aren't always going to be bad all the time

Forgiveness

In what areas of life are you must judgmental?

In what I think is right and wrong behavior

How my wife/girlfriend acts

Other people's religion and politics

Why do you feel you have the right interpretation?

Because I don't take the time to walk a while in the other person's shoes

Because I'm insecure about how I'm doing and how I'm seeing the situation

What is an issue in your life you could view with a different perspective?

All the events in my past that I have given a negative interpretation to; I feel I could change much of my past if I could revisit it with understanding forgiveness, and integrity

What it means to have an intimate relationship

Love

Discuss love as an emotion.

Love is a word with many different meanings. I love chocolate, I love my dog, I love my job, and I love my partner. Obviously, I don't love all four of them in the same way or with the same intensity—just because I use the same word in all cases.

Love is a mighty powerful emotion when you extend it to others with integrity, patience, flexibility, gratitude, nonviolence, understanding, and forgiveness. When love is the filter through which we see the world, it changes the world before our very eyes. It's the positive opposite to the urge to take an eye for an eye . . . which only leaves everyone blind and lost.

How is love influenced by the person giving love? By the person who is receiving the love?
The power and potential of love is influenced by the motive of the lover and the needs of the person receiving the love. That's why the most fulfilling and useful love is infused with integrity, patience, flexibility, gratitude, nonviolence, understanding, and forgiveness.

What difference, if any, do you see between the function of love and the art of love?
Seeing and practicing love as just a function makes it mechanical and shallow. We don't get to know the person we love, but instead see them as an object—like real estate we want to develop or exploit. Real love is an art that allows (and encourages!) both people to develop and grow in the ongoing, creative and beautiful mystery of love.

Acknowledgments

The authors are deeply grateful to the following people, and many others unnamed, for their help in bringing to reality this workbook and the Positive Attitude Development program.

John Clark Pegg	Nancy Gruver	Tina Mandeville
Lyn Clark Pegg	Bill Wilson	Danny Ross
Coral McDonnell	Bill Klatte	Glen Rois
Brooks Anderson	Nikki Jo Woseth	Todd Smith
Frank Renzo	Paul LeRose	Stewert Van Maasdam
Frank Jewell	Rob Evina	Christopher Motter
Henry Moore	Leo Piatz	Jeremiah Mathews
Scott Miller	Kathy Piatz	Tom Halloran
Ruth Stricker	Jeff Jurkens	
Dan L. Bayes	Dan Kaufman	

For more information, visit
www.PADgroup.org or email **info@PADgroup.org.**

Printed in the United States
143633LV00003BA/1/P

9 781570 252280